W9-CAT-277

See back of book for signatures & how much you accomplished!

Wolf
Handbook

Welcome to the Wolf Handbook!

I am Akela. I will be your leader and friend. I will guide you along the Wolf trail.

Illustrations of Akela by Robert Depew

33450
ISBN 978-0-8395-3450-1
©2003 Boy Scouts of America
2011 Printing

GATE/Louisville, KY
6-2011/062110

Contents

Arrow Point Trail (Electives)

Trail Summary

How to help your son follow the Bobcat, Wolf, and Arrow Point trails

If you could give your son the greatest gift of all, what would it be? It wouldn't be money or anything money can buy. Whether you are rich or poor, the greatest gift is within your power because that gift helps a boy become a person with a good feeling about himself and a genuine concern for others. Cub Scouting can help you provide this gift.

Your Son, Cub Scouting, and You

As a parent or guardian, you want your son to grow up to be self-reliant and dependable—a person of worth, a caring individual. Scouting has these same goals in mind for him.

Since 1910 we've been weaving lifetime values into fun and educational activities designed to help families teach their boys how to make good decisions throughout their lives and give them confidence as they become the adult leaders of tomorrow.

In a society where your son is often taught that winning is everything, Cub Scouting teaches him to do his best and be helpful to others as expressed in the Cub Scout Promise, motto, and Law of the Pack.

The Wolf den will involve your son in a group of boys his own age where he can earn status and recognition. There he will also gain a sense of personal achievement from the new skills he learns.

The Purposes of Cub Scouting

Cub Scouting is a year-round family-oriented part of the BSA program designed for boys who are in first through fifth grades (or are 7, 8, 9, and 10 years old). Parents, leaders, and organizations work together to achieve the 10 purposes of Cub Scouting:

1. Character Development
2. Spiritual Growth
3. Good Citizenship
4. Sportsmanship and Fitness
5. Family Understanding
6. Respectful Relationships
7. Personal Achievement
8. Friendly Service
9. Fun and Adventure
10. Preparation for Boy Scouts

Cub Scouting

Your Cub Scout is a member of a Wolf Cub Scout den. Most dens have six to eight boys and meet once a week. Den meetings are a time for learning new things and having fun. Dens are led by a team of adult volunteers—the den leader and assistant den leader(s). Den leaders are usually adult family members of boys in the den.

Your Cub Scout is also a member of a pack. Most packs have several dens and meet once a month. Pack meetings usually follow a suggested theme and are a time for boys to be recognized for their accomplishments during the month, to perform skits and songs they've learned in den meetings, and to have fun with the entire family.

Packs are led by a Cubmaster and pack committee. Like the den leaders, the Cubmaster and assistants are volunteers and are usually adult family members of boys in the pack. Most pack committees consist of adult family members and members of the pack's chartered organization. The pack committee makes plans for pack meetings and activities and takes care of the "business" items necessary for a quality pack program.

The pack is owned by a community organization that is granted a charter by the Boy Scouts of America to use the Scouting program. This chartered organization might be a school, service club, religious group, or other group interested in youth. The chartered organization approves the leadership of the pack, provides a meeting place, and operates the pack within the guidelines and policies of the organization and the Boy Scouts of America.

Akela's OK

As you look through this book, you'll see places for "Akela's OK." That usually means your okay. Akela (ah-KAY-la) is the boy's leader. At home, that is you; at den meetings, it is the den leader; at school, it is the teacher. Almost all electives and achievements are done by you and your Cub Scout at home, not in the den meeting. This book is filled with more than 200 pages of activities for you and your son to enjoy together. Once your Cub Scout has done his best, you can approve the completion of the requirement and the den leader will record his progress in the den records.

	Mary Dunning	*[date here]*	*Matt Douglas*
1	BOBCAT TRAIL	Akela's OK	Date	Recorded by the den leader

Notes for Akela

Throughout the *Wolf Handbook*, special notes for you are printed along with the requirements for special projects that require the supervision and participation of adults. Watch for these "Notes for Akela." They are printed in a smaller, different typestyle for your easy identification. This is an example:

> NOTE for Akela: This is a note for the parent or other adult helping a Wolf Cub Scout along the trail.

Character Connections®

Cub Scouting's Character Connections program helps your son *know, commit,* and *practice* Cub Scouting's 12 core values while enjoying fun and adventure in his Wolf den. This symbol identifies Character Connections throughout this book and in other Cub Scouting materials.

Cub Scouting's 12 Core Values

1. **Citizenship:** Contributing service and showing responsibility to local, state, and national communities.

2. **Compassion:** Being kind and considerate, and showing concern for the well-being of others.

3. **Cooperation:** Being helpful and working together with others toward a common goal.

4. **Courage:** Being brave and doing what is right regardless of our fears, the difficulties, or the consequences.

5. **Faith:** Having inner strength and confidence based on our trust in God.

6. **Health and Fitness:** Being personally committed to keeping our minds and bodies clean and fit.

7. **Honesty:** Telling the truth and being worthy of trust.

8. **Perseverance:** Sticking with something and not giving up, even if it is difficult.

9. **Positive Attitude:** Being cheerful and setting our minds to look for and find the best in all situations.

10. **Resourcefulness**: Using human and other resources to their fullest.

11. **Respect:** Showing regard for the worth of something or someone.

12. **Responsibility:** Fulfilling our duty to God, country, other people, and ourselves.

The Bobcat Trail

In Rudyard Kipling's *The Jungle Book*, the black panther Begheera is the mighty hunter who teaches the cubs the skills of the jungle. In Cub Scouting we use the symbol of the Bobcat. The Bobcat rank is for all boys who join Cub Scouting. If your boy joined Cub Scouting as a Wolf Cub Scout, he must earn the Bobcat badge before receiving any other award or rank. You'll find his trail (the requirements) on pages 16 through 35. Along this trail are the Cub Scout Promise, the Law of the Pack, and the Cub Scout motto. These are the three most important things a boy must learn because they will help him through all of the trails of Scouting.

One part of the Bobcat trail is to read and complete the exercises in the booklet *How to Protect Your Children from Child Abuse*. Child abuse is a problem in our society, and this booklet will help you help your child to avoid potentially abusive situations. **Note**: The booklet is provided as a a tear-out section in the front of this book. Please do tear it out (that makes the book easier to handle), read it carefully, and keep it at hand for easy reference.

When you and your son have followed the eight tracks of the Bobcat, he may wear his Bobcat badge. It will be presented at the pack meeting.

The Wolf Trail

After your Cub Scout has earned his Bobcat badge, he can start along the Wolf trail. This is a big adventure for a boy, one the Boy Scouts of America hopes all boys will complete.

When you have okayed the tracks your son has filled in for all 12 achievements, he may become a Wolf Cub Scout. How quickly your son progresses is up to him and you. He should do his best to complete each track; that's a part of the promise he made to become a Bobcat and it is the Cub Scout motto—Do Your Best. Don't okay a track if you both know that he can do a better job. Move on to something else, then go back and try again.

The important thing is to keep him interested by working on the trail with him as often as possible.

Progress Toward Ranks

Your son doesn't have to wait until he completes his entire Wolf trail before being recognized for his work. When he completes any three achievements, his den leader can present the Progress Toward Ranks emblem to him. It's a diamond with a plastic thong, and is worn on the button of the right pocket of his uniform shirt. Each time he completes three achievements he will receive another gold bead. After he gets his fourth gold bead, he will be ready to receive his Wolf badge at a pack meeting.

The Arrow Point Trail

Your Cub Scout can also search the Arrow Point trail. On the Wolf trail, the main sections were called achievements, things that we would like all boys to do. On the Arrow Point trail, the main sections are called electives, choices that a boy can make on his own and with your guidance.

To earn a Gold Arrow Point to wear beneath his Wolf badge, a boy must complete any 10 elective projects of the more than 100 choices shown in the book. For every 10 additional electives he completes, the Wolf Cub Scout qualifies for a Silver Arrow Point to wear beneath the Gold. He can earn as many Silver Arrow Points as he wants until he completes the second grade (or turns 9). Arrow Points are presented at the pack meeting after he receives his Wolf badge.

Your son should begin earning achievements toward his Wolf badge as soon as he completes the Bobcat requirements. Completing electives for Arrow Points generally should wait until after he has earned his Wolf badge, and he cannot receive Arrow Points until he has been awarded his Wolf badge. He might, however, find some electives that he could be completing before he earns the Wolf badge. Some of the activities in "Sports," Wolf Elective 20, might be examples. As long as he completes these electives after he has earned his Bobcat, you may credit him for them, but be sure to keep him focused on the 12 achievements until he completes them.

a

Mary Duning   *[date here]*   _Matt Douglas_
Arrow Point Trail   Akela's OK   Date   Recorded by the den leader

Do Your Best

When has a boy completed an elective or achievement? When he, in your opinion as Akela, has completed the skill to the best of his ability. In Cub Scouting, boys are judged against their own standard, not against other boys.

If your Cub Scout has a mental or physical disability that prevents him from attempting an achievement, talk to your Cubmaster about using an elective as an alternative.

The Story of Akela and Mowgli

Baden-Powell, the founder of Scouting, based Cub Scouting on one of the stories in Rudyard Kipling's *Jungle Book*. It was called "Mowgli's Brothers." We know it as "The Story of Akela and Mowgli." Read the story twice, once to yourself and the second time to your Cub Scout.

Once upon a time in the jungles of India on a warm summer evening, Father Wolf awoke, stretched his paws, and prepared to go hunting.

The moon shone into the mouth of the cave where Mother Wolf lay sleeping with their four young cubs. Suddenly, a shadow crossed the opening of the cave and a whining voice said, "Good hunting, o' chief of the wolves, and good luck to your children." It was Tabaqui, the sneaky little jackal who, because he is too lazy to hunt for himself, picks up scraps left by other animals.

Father Wolf told him, "There is no food here, but come in if you wish."

Tabaqui said, "For a poor animal like myself a dry bone is a feast," and in no time at all he was cracking away on a bone at the back of the cave. Now Tabaqui was always ready to make trouble and to talk about others. He said, "Shere Khan, the mighty tiger, has changed his hunting ground. He hunts in these hills for the next moon." (Shere Khan was the tiger who lived about 20 miles away, near the big river.)

Father Wolf said, "By the Law of the Jungle, he has no right to change his hunting ground. He will scare the animals away for miles around."

Tabaqui said, "I could have saved myself the trouble of telling you. You can hear him now in the jungle below." And he trotted off to find the tiger.

Father and Mother Wolf listened. From the valley below, they could hear the angry whine of a tiger who had caught nothing and didn't care if the whole jungle knew it.

"The fool," said Father Wolf, "to start a night's hunting with all that noise!" The whine changed to a humming-purr, which is the noise a tiger makes when he is hunting humans. Father Wolf said, "Are there not enough frogs and beetles that he must hunt humans?"

Just then there was a most untigerish howl from Shere Khan, and Mother Wolf said, "He missed! What happened?"

Father Wolf ran out a few paces and looked down to a clearing where there were several woodcutters' huts. He said, "Shere Khan has had no more sense than to jump at the woodcutters' fire. He burned his feet! Tabaqui is with him and they have frightened all the people away."

"Listen," Mother Wolf said, "something is coming up the hill. Get ready!"

Father Wolf crouched and sprang, but as he sprang, he stopped himself in midair because what he saw was a little boy!

"Man!" he said. "A man-cub. Look!"

"I have never seen one," Mother Wolf said. "Bring him to me."

Father Wolf brought him into the cave and put him down beside Mother Wolf. The boy snuggled close to the young wolf cubs. "How little he is," said Mother Wolf.

Suddenly, the moonlight was blocked from the door of the cave by the great head and shoulders of Shere Khan.

"What does Shere Khan want?" said Father Wolf with angry eyes.

"The man-cub!" said Shere Khan. "Give him to me!"

Father Wolf said, "The wolves take orders only from Akela, the head of the wolf pack. The man-cub is ours."

The tiger's roar filled the cave with thunder. "The man-cub is mine. Give him to me!" said Shere Khan.

Mother Wolf sprang up quickly and said, "The man-cub is ours. You have frightened his family away. He shall not be killed. He shall live to run with the pack and hunt with the pack."

Shere Khan knew he could not fight the two wolves in the cave; therefore, he went away growling, snarling, and saying, "We will see what the pack has to say about this man-cub."

When the tiger had gone, Father Wolf said, "Shere Khan is right. What will the pack say?" But Mother Wolf had decided to keep him. And they called him Mowgli ("the frog") because his skin was smooth and without hair. Mowgli stayed with the young cubs.

When they were old enough to run, Father and Mother Wolf set off with them one night, through the jungle to a meeting of the wolf pack at the Council Rock. The Law of the Jungle states that wolves must gather to look over the new wolf cubs of the pack, so that they will know them and take care of them when they see them in the jungle.

As each young wolf was pushed into the circle, Akela, the great leader of the wolf pack, sitting high on the Council Rock, called, "Look at each cub, o' wolves. Look well." At last it was Mowgli's turn and Mother Wolf pushed him into the circle where he sat playing with some stones in the moonlight. Akela did not even twitch an ear as he called, "Look well, o' wolves."

From outside the circle came a roar from Shere Khan. "The man-cub is mine. Give him to me." Some of the wolves took up the cry, "What do we want with a man-cub in the pack?"

There is a law that says if there is an argument as to the right of a cub to join the pack, two members must speak for him. Akela asked, "Who speaks for this cub?"

At first there was no answer, but then Baloo, the sleepy brown bear who teaches the cubs the Law of the Pack, stepped into the circle

and said, "I will speak for the man-cub. Let him join the pack and I, myself, will teach him the law and the ways of the jungle."

"We need another," said Akela. "Who besides Baloo speaks?"

An inky black shadow dropped silently into the circle. It was Bagheera, the black panther, the mighty hunter who teaches the cubs the skills of the jungle. In his soft silky voice he said, "If there is a question about the right of a cub to join the pack, his life may be bought at a price. Isn't that the law?"

"Yes," said the pack.

"Then to Baloo's good word, I will add fresh meat which is in the valley below, if you will accept Mowgli into the pack."

The wolves cried, "Let him join. What harm can a man-cub do?" They looked him over; then, one by one, the wolves went down the hill, leaving Mowgli with Father and Mother Wolf, Baloo, and Bagheera at the Council Rock with Akela. Akela said, "Now take him away and teach him the Law of the Pack."

And that is how Mowgli joined the Seeonee Wolf Pack.

The Boy Scouts of America hereby authorizes you, who have read this Parent Guide, to act as Akela. Indicate your willingness to serve by signing below.

I/We will be Akela in this
Wolf Handbook:

Signature _____ Date _____

Signature _____ Date _____

Signature _____ Date _____

Welcome to the Wolf Cub Scout Den!

You have heard how Mowgli met Akela (say ah-KAY-la). Just as that story says, in a real wolf pack all the wolves look to Akela, the leader, for guidance—when to work, when to learn, when to play.

Akela makes sure each young wolf in the pack gets the chance to learn about the world, and how to get along with other members of the pack.

There are times when Akela romps and plays games with members of the pack. But there are times when Akela, with a movement of his head or a steady gaze, commands the young wolves' attention.

Akela, the wolf pack leader, is caring and wise. He is both a friend and a teacher.

Like your parents or guardians, your teachers, and other adults who help you learn, Akela is your guide.

Throughout the pages of this book, Akela will guide you to your place in the pack. Along the Wolf trail, you will learn the Cub Scout Promise and the Law of the Pack.

You will learn new skills. You will try new things. Akela, your guide, will help you begin your exciting trail through Cub Scouting, and onward to the Webelos den.

Come! Be a part of the pack. Follow the trail.

We begin our trail by following Akela's friend, the Bobcat. If you have not earned your Bobcat badge yet, follow his trail first to become a Bobcat Cub Scout and to earn your place in the pack.

Bobcat Trail

Welcome to Our Pack!

Say hi to my friend the Bobcat. He has eight things for you to do.

HE SAYS

"Follow my Bobcat Trail."

Fill in this track when you have completed all the Bobcat tracks. You may also mark the Trail Summary on page 233. When you have filled in all eight tracks, you can wear the Bobcat badge.

1 Learn and say the Cub Scout Promise and complete the Honesty Character Connection.

Cub Scout Promise

I, . . V.l. . d. . . ϵ. . ϵ. . , ye n

promise to do my best
To do my duty to God and
my country,
To help other people, and
To obey the Law of the Pack.

When you say you will do something, that is a *promise*.

Duty to God means:
Put God first. Do what you know God wants you to do.

And my country means:
Do what you can for your country. Be proud that you are an American.

To help other people means:
Do things for others that would help them.

Obey the Law of the Pack means:
Do what Akela asks you to do. Be a good Cub Scout. Be proud that you are one.

Honesty

Know. Discuss these questions with your family: What is a promise? What does it mean to "keep your word?" What does *honesty* mean? What does it mean to "do your best?"

Commit. Discuss these questions with your family. Why is a promise important? Why is it important for people to trust you when you give your word? When might it be difficult to keep your word? List examples.

Practice. Discuss with family members why it is important to be trustworthy and honest and how you can do your best to be honest when you are doing the activities in Cub Scouting.

When you can say the Cub Scout Promise and have completed the Honesty Character Connection on this page, fill in my track.

OK   (0-28-2011)

Akela's OK   Date   Recorded by the den leader

The Law of the Pack

The Cub Scout follows Akela.
The Cub Scout helps the pack go.
The pack helps the Cub Scout grow.
The Cub Scout gives goodwill.

The Cub Scout follows Akela (say Ah-KAY-la).

Akela is a good leader.
Your mother or father or other adult member of your family is Akela.
In the pack, your Cubmaster is Akela.
Your den leader is Akela.
At school, your teacher is Akela.

The Cub Scout helps the pack go.

Come to all the meetings. Do what you can to help. Think of others in the pack.

The pack helps the Cub Scout grow.

You can have fun when you are a part of the pack. Learn things from others. Do things with them.

The Cub Scout gives goodwill.

Smile. Be happy. Do things to help others. Little things make a big difference.

When you can say the Law of the Pack and tell what it means, fill in my track.

OK   10-29-11
_____   _____   _____
Akela's OK   Date   Recorded by the den leader

Webelos

Webelos (say WE-buh-lows) has a special meaning that Cub Scouts know. It is <u>We</u>'ll <u>Be</u> <u>Lo</u>yal <u>S</u>couts.

We'll
Be
Loyal
Scouts
} # WeBeLoS

Being loyal means that you will keep the Cub Scout Promise.

The Webelos Arrow of Light points the right way to go every day of the week. That is why the sun has seven rays—one for each day.

When you can tell what *Webelos* means, fill in my track.

3

_ol<u>C</u>_____ _12-27-11_____ _____
Akela's OK   Date   Recorded by the den leader

Make the Cub Scout sign with your right hand. Hold with your arm straight up.

Cub Scout Sign

The two fingers stand for two parts of the Promise—"to help other people" and "to obey." They look like a wolf's ears; this means you are ready to listen to Akela.

Give the Cub Scout sign when you say the Cub Scout Promise or the Law of the Pack.

When you can give the Cub Scout sign and tell what it means, fill in my track.

__OK_____ __10-27-11__ _____
Akela's OK   Date   Recorded by the den leader

5 Show the Cub Scout handshake. Tell what it means.

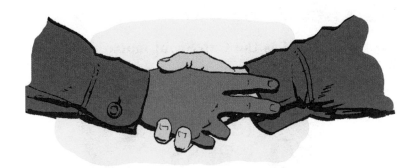

Cub Scout Handshake

Here's how to shake hands with another Cub Scout. Hold out your right hand just as you always do to shake hands. Put your first two fingers along the inside of the other boy's wrist.

This means that you help and that you obey the Law of the Pack.

When you can shake hands as a Cub Scout and tell what the handshake means, fill in my track.

5

_OK_   _10-27-11_

Akela's OK   Date   Recorded by the den leader

Cub Scout Motto

DO YOUR BEST is the Cub Scout motto.

It means

When you play a game, do your best to help your team.

When you study in school, do your best to learn from your teacher.

When you help at home, do your best to help your family.
Whatever you do, do your best.

When you know the Cub Scout motto and can tell what it means, fill in my track.

6

_OK_   10-28-2011

Akela's OK   Date   Recorded by the den leader

7 Give the Cub Scout salute.
Tell what it means.

Cub Scout Salute

A salute is a way to show respect. We salute the flag to show respect to our country.

For the Cub Scout salute, use your right hand. Hold your fingers as you do for the Cub Scout sign. Keep the two straight fingers close together. Touch the tips of those fingers to your cap. If you are not wearing a cap, touch your right eyebrow.

When you can give the Cub Scout salute and tell what it means, fill in my track.

Akela's OK   10-28-2011   Recorded by the den leader
                    Date

Child Protection Exercises

When you have completed these exercises with your parent or guardian, fill in my track.

8

oK 10-30-2011

Akela's OK   Date   Recorded by the den leader

Your Den

Your den is a group of boys who live in your general neighborhood. You might know and play with most of them.

About once a week you will meet with your den. Your den leader, the adult in charge of the meetings, will be Akela.

Your den leader will help guide you through the exciting Wolf trail that is part of the Cub Scout adventure. You will have fun doing that and other things.

You and other boys in your den will have fun getting ready for the pack meeting in many of your den meetings.

Cub Scouting is fun, and much of that fun starts in your den.

The den meeting is usually held in somebody's home. It might be held in your home.

What do you do at a den meeting? Lots of things. You'd better be on time or you will miss something.

When you get there, Cub Scouts might be playing a game or doing a puzzle.

When all the Cub Scouts are there, it is time to start the meeting.

You might salute the flag or say the Cub Scout Promise.

Maybe you will play a game that has something to do with the month's theme. Or you could do a stunt or skit or make something.

Before the meeting ends, you might be a part of the Living Circle ceremony. Hold out your left hand—palm down and thumb out. Hold the thumb of the boy on your left.

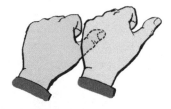

DO	SAY
Raise the Living Circle.	AH
Lower it.	KAY
Raise it.	LA
Lower it.	WE'LL
Raise it.	DO
Lower it.	OUR
Raise it.	BEST

Or you might end the meeting with this Cub Scout closing in sign language.

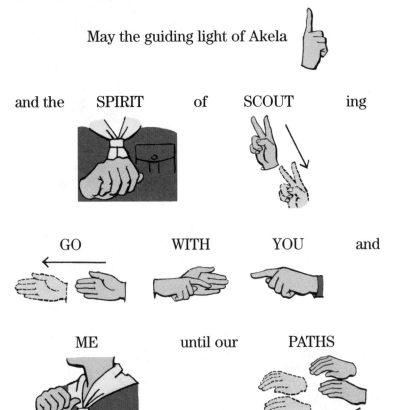

May the guiding light of Akela

and the SPIRIT of SCOUT ing

GO WITH YOU and

ME until our PATHS

cross again.

Before you leave the den meeting, do three things:

1. Help clean up the room.
2. Be sure you have all your things.
3. Thank Akela (your leader).

Go home and get ready for more fun.

Your Pack

You will meet members of other dens at a pack meeting.

A pack meeting includes a show that has a theme, such as Cub Scout fair, or blue and gold banquet. Each den takes a part in the show.

But pack meetings are not just for Cub Scouts. Pack meetings are for families. They watch while Tiger Cubs, you and other Cub Scouts, and Webelos Scouts do your stuff and get your badges.

Your pack might belong to a church or a school or something like that. Your pack meets there.

The pack leader is called a Cubmaster. The Cubmaster is Akela for the pack.

Your Uniform

Now that you are a Cub Scout, you get to wear a uniform like the one shown on this page and page 35. It has blue pants or shorts and a blue shirt. There is a blue belt with a Cub Scout buckle, and a blue and gold neckerchief with a slide. You also wear an official navy blue cap with gold front panel and Wolf emblem.

You will earn lots of badges as a Cub Scout. These pictures show where to wear them on your uniform shirt.

World Crest

Temporary patch area

Right pocket

Left pocket

Right sleeve

Left sleeve

Roll your neckerchief before you put it on. Here's how:

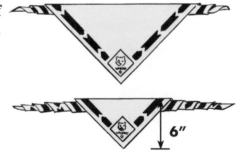

6″

The Blue and Gold

The blue in your uniform stands for truth and spirituality, steadfast loyalty, and the sky above. Gold stands for warm sunlight, good cheer, and happiness. When you wear the Cub Scout uniform, people will know you are trying to be good and helpful.

Wear It

Wear your uniform to den and pack meetings. Wear it whenever you take part in something Cub Scouts do. Keep your uniform clean and neat. Hang it in a closet or fold it and put it in a drawer or on a shelf.

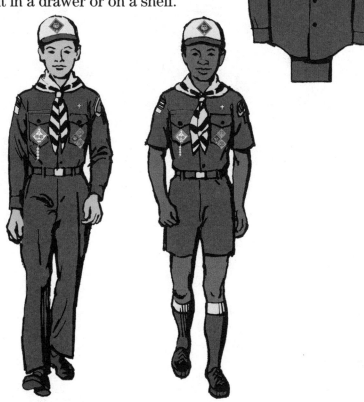

Now, follow my
Wolf Trail

My track is different from the Bobcat's. Cats don't show their claws, but wolves and dogs do.

Bobcat

Wolf

Fill in my tracks as you follow my trail. This will help you keep track of your progress along the Wolf trail. Not all the tracks have to be filled in. Sometimes you can choose. You may also fill in the tracks on the Trail Summary on pages 233 and 234.

1 Feats of Skill

You are growing. You are getting stronger. Try these feats of skill. Test your speed. Test your balance. Test your strength.

1a

Play catch with someone 10 steps away. Play until you can throw and catch.

_____   _____   _____
Akela's OK   Date   Recorded by the den leader

REQUIREMENT

1b

Walk a line back and forth. Do it sideways, too. Then walk the edge of a board six steps each way.

_____   _____   _____
Akela's OK   Date   Recorded by the den leader

NOTE for Akela: If a physician certifies that a Cub Scout's physical condition for an indeterminable time won't permit him to do three of these requirements, the Cubmaster and pack committee may authorize substitution of any three Arrow Point electives.

Achievement 1

1c Do a front roll.

Akela's OK   Date   Recorded by the den leader

1d Do a back roll.

Akela's OK   Date   Recorded by the den leader

1e Do a falling forward roll.

Akela's OK   Date   Recorded by the den leader

Do ONE of the following (f, g, h, i, j, k, or l).
DO THIS ⬅️

 1f

See how high you can jump.

Prepare to blast off. Coil your body and then count down from 10 to zero.

When you come to zero, yell "Blast-off!" and jump as high into the air as you can. Land on your feet.

Akela's OK   Date   Recorded by the den leader

1g Do the elephant walk, frog leap, and crab walk.

Elephant walk

Frog leap

Crab walk

| Akela's OK | Date | Recorded by the den leader |

Wolf Trail

REQUIREMENT

1h

Using a basic swim stroke, swim 25 feet.

Do this in shallow water with a grown-up who swims well.

NOTE for Akela: Measure at the side of the pool, or along the shore of a pond or lake.

Akela's OK	Date	Recorded by the den leader

NOTE for Akela: Check with the den leader or Cubmaster and be sure your Cub Scout follows all procedures of Safe Swim Defense when participating in any swimming, boating, or water activity.

REQUIREMENT

1i

Tread water for 15 seconds or as long as you can. Do your best.

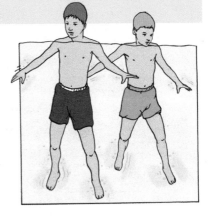

Akela's OK   Date   Recorded by the den leader

REQUIREMENT

1j

Using a basketball or playground ball, do a—

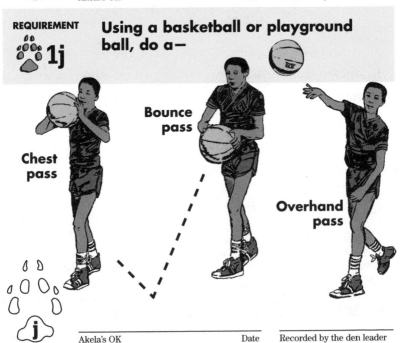

Chest pass

Bounce pass

Overhand pass

Akela's OK   Date   Recorded by the den leader

OR THIS

REQUIREMENT 1k

Do a frog stand.

Akela's OK   Date   Recorded by the den leader

REQUIREMENT 11

Run or jog in place for 5 minutes.

Akela's OK   Date   Recorded by the den leader

The United States flag stands for our country. Learn some ways to honor your flag.

Give the Pledge of Allegiance to the flag of the United States of America. Tell what it means.

Pledge of Allegiance

> **I pledge allegiance
> to the flag of the
> United States of America
> and to the republic
> for which it stands,
> one nation under God,
> indivisible, with liberty
> and justice for all.**

A **pledge** is a promise.

Allegiance is to be true.

Republic is our kind of government.

Nation is a country.

God is the one we worship.

Indivisible is one that cannot be divided into pieces or parts.

Liberty is freedom for you and for others.

Justice is what is right and fair.

Akela's OK	Date	Recorded by the den leader

**Lead a flag ceremony in your den.
Here are some ideas:**

Get your den to stand in a straight line and face the U.S. flag. Salute and say the Pledge of Allegiance.

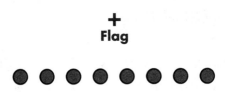

OR

Stand in a square formation. Bring in the U.S. flag. Salute and say the Cub Scout Promise.

OR

Stand in a circle around the U.S. flag. Salute and say the Pledge of Allegiance.

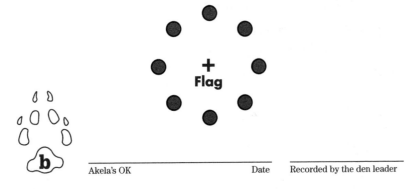

Akela's OK   Date   Recorded by the den leader

REQUIREMENT

Tell how to respect and take care of the U.S. flag. Show three ways to display it.

Be careful **not** to

1. Let the flag get dirty.

2. Let the flag get torn.

3. Let the flag touch the ground.

Can you think of other ways to care for your flag?

Display the flag inside

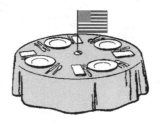

and outside from your windows.

Akela's OK	Date	Recorded by the den leader

Learn about the flag of your state or territory and how to display it.

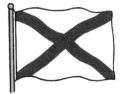

ALABAMA

ALASKA

AMERICAN SAMOA

ARIZONA

ARKANSAS

CALIFORNIA

COLORADO

CONNECTICUT

DELAWARE

DISTRICT OF COLUMBIA

FLORIDA

GEORGIA

GUAM

HAWAII

IDAHO

ILLINOIS

INDIANA

IOWA

KANSAS

KENTUCKY

LOUISIANA

MAINE

MARYLAND

MASSACHUSETTS

MICHIGAN

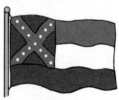

MINNESOTA

MISSISSIPPI

MISSOURI

MONTANA

NEBRASKA

NEVADA

NEW HAMPSHIRE

NEW JERSEY

NEW MEXICO

NEW YORK

NORTH CAROLINA

NORTH DAKOTA

OHIO

OKLAHOMA

OREGON

PENNSYLVANIA

PUERTO RICO

RHODE ISLAND

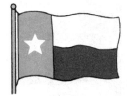

SOUTH CAROLINA

SOUTH DAKOTA

TENNESSEE

TEXAS

UTAH

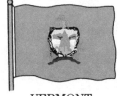

VERMONT

VIRGIN ISLANDS

VIRGINIA

Wolf Trail

WASHINGTON

WEST VIRGINIA

WISCONSIN

WYOMING

**Displaying the state
flag with U.S. flag
and pack flag**

Learn how to raise a U.S. flag properly for an outdoor ceremony.

Always salute as the U.S. flag is being raised or lowered on a flagpole. After it is down, fold it and put it in a safe place.

Akela's OK   Date   Recorded by the den leader

Participate in an outdoor flag ceremony.

Akela's OK   Date   Recorded by the den leader

With the help of another person, fold the U.S. flag.

Fold once.

Then fold again.

Fold corner up and over.

Now fold down.

Keep folding until it looks like this.

Tuck the end in here. →

When the U.S. flag is folded correctly, it looks like the three-cornered hats worn during the American Revolutionary War and no red shows.

Akela's OK   Date   Recorded by the den leader

3 Keep Your Body Healthy

Be healthy and strong. Learn what to do to be healthy.
Keep active to be strong.

Make a chart and keep track of your health habits for two weeks.

On your chart, show how you follow these habits of good health:

- **Bathe or shower often; use soap.** Do this once a day, if you can. Mark on your chart when you do.
- **Wash your hands** before meals and after you use the toilet. Chart how many times a day you do this.
- **Brush your teeth** before you go to bed and after breakfast, and then mark it on your chart. Also brush your teeth or rinse your mouth after you eat.
- **Drink lots of water**—six or eight glasses every day. You could draw a little glass on your chart for every glass you drink.
- **Run and play outdoors,** but protect yourself from the sun. Use sunscreen. Wear a hat. (See the guidelines on page 196.) Chart how many minutes you are outdoors every day.
- **Get the sleep you need.** Chart how many hours you sleep each night.

Akela's OK _____ Date _____ Recorded by the den leader

Tell four ways to stop the spread of colds.

1. If you have a cold, stay away from other people.

2. Get lots of rest.

3. Turn your head away from others when you sneeze or cough. Cover your mouth and nose.

4. Wash your hands often, and always wash them after you sneeze.

_____   _____   _____
Akela's OK   Date   Recorded by the den leader

1. Tell a grown-up about the cut.

2. Let the cut bleed a little.

3. Wash it with soap and water.

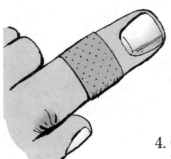

4. Cover it with a stick-on bandage. For a big cut, get help fast.

Akela's OK _____   Date _____   Recorded by the den leader

Strive to do your best at home. Being responsible will help you be happy and safe. You should know what to do in case of emergency. Here are some things you should know and do whether you are home with your family or home alone. Taking care of yourself is a good way to be responsible and helpful in your home.

Make a list of phone numbers you need in case of an emergency. Put a copy of this list by each phone or in a central place in your home. Update it often.

Include on your list the phone numbers for

- The police department
- The sheriff
- The fire department
- A doctor
- An ambulance service
- Adult family member (or members) at work
- Relatives at home
- Neighbors

Can you think of other important numbers?

Learn whether the 9-1-1 emergency service is available in your area and know how to use it if it is.

Ask an adult in your family to teach you how to use all the different kinds of phones you might have in your house, such as a cell phone or a pager.

| _____ | | _____ | _____ |
| Akela's OK | | Date | Recorded by the den leader |

Tell what to do if someone comes to the door and wants to come in.

NOTE for Akela: Discuss with your boy what to do if someone wants to come in when your boy is home alone.

| _____ | | _____ | _____ |
| Akela's OK | | Date | Recorded by the den leader |

4c Tell what to do if someone calls on the phone.

NOTE for Akela: Discuss with your boy what to say if someone calls and your boy is home alone.

c

Akela's OK _____ Date _____ Recorded by the den leader

4d When you and your family leave home, remember to...

_____ Turn off the lights.

_____ Close and lock the windows.

_____ Turn off the water.

_____ Take care of pets.

_____ Have my key.

_____ Lock all of the doors.

NOTE for Akela: Help your boy to make sure everything is taken care of before he leaves the house.

d

Akela's OK _____ Date _____ Recorded by the den leader

4e

Talk with your family members. Agree on the household jobs you will be responsible for. Make a list of your jobs and mark off when you have finished them. Do this for one month.

NOTE for Akela: You can teach your boy responsibility by helping him find jobs he can do to help around the home.

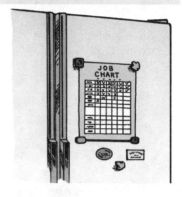

Akela's OK	Date	Recorded by the den leader

4f

Visit an important place in your community, such as a historic or government location. Explain why it is important.

Akela's OK	Date	Recorded by the den leader

Achievement 5

Tools for Fixing and Building

You can make something if you know how to use tools. You can fix things that are broken.

Point out and name seven tools. Do this at home, or go to a hardware store with an adult. Tell what each tool does.

C-clamp to hold things in place

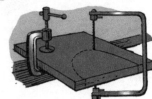

Coping saw for cutting curves in wood

Handsaw for straight cuts in wood

Claw hammer to drive nails and pull them out

Hacksaw to cut metal

File to smooth metal

Awl to punch holes

Plane to smooth wood

Adjustable wrench to turn bolts or nuts

Akela's OK

Date   Recorded by the den leader

Show how to use pliers.

Slip-joint pliers

Slip the joint this way for small jobs.

Slip the joint this way for big jobs.

Needle Nose Pliers

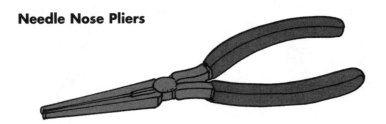

These are used to hold very small parts.

_____
Akela's OK   Date   Recorded by the den leader

Identify a Phillips head and a standard screw. Then use the right tool to drive and then remove one from a board.

1. Start a hole in the wood with an awl or a nail.

2. A screw with soap on it is easier to turn.

3. Twist the screw into the hole.

4. Pick the right screwdriver to fit the screw.

5. Turn the screw until the head is in the wood.

Akela's OK   Date   Recorded by the den leader

Show how to use a hammer.

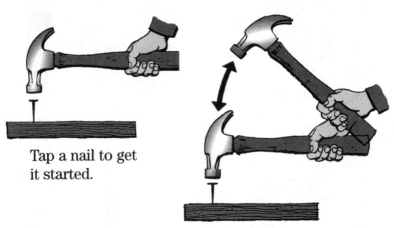

Tap a nail to get it started.

Lift up the hammer and drop it on the nail. Let the hammer do the work.

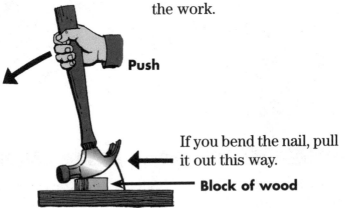

Push

If you bend the nail, pull it out this way.

Block of wood

| Akela's OK | | Date | Recorded by the den leader |

Make a birdhouse, a set of bookends, or something else useful.

NOTE for Akela: Birdhouse kits and other projects are available at your local Scout shop.

Akela's OK   Date   Recorded by the den leader

6 Start a Collection

You can collect almost anything. Put your collection together so that you can show it to your family, den, and pack.

Positive Attitude

Know. Discuss with your family how a cheerful and positive attitude will help you to do your best at school and in other areas of your life.

Commit. Discuss with your family how gathering items for a collection may be difficult. How does a hopeful and cheerful attitude help you to keep looking for more items? Why is a positive attitude important?

Practice. Practice having a positive attitude while doing the requirements for "Start a Collection."

_____   _____   _____
Akela's OK   Date   Recorded by the den leader

REQUIREMENT

6b

Make a collection of anything you like. Start with 10 things. Put them together in a neat way.

Use an empty egg carton for stones or things like that.

Hold shells in place with wire or glue.

Use stamp hinges to put stamps in a book or use clear plastic holders.

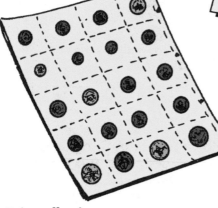

Coin collection

Patch collection

Wolf Trail

Leaf collection

Only collect leaves that have already fallen from trees or bushes.

b

_____ _____ _____
Akela's OK   Date   Recorded by the den leader

REQUIREMENT
6c

Show and explain your collection to another person.

I showed and explained my collection to _____

_____

_____

c

_____ _____ _____
Akela's OK   Date   Recorded by the den leader

7 Your Living World

Our world is the only one we have. Take care of it. There are many ways you can help.

This achievement is also part of the Cub Scout World Conservation Award and Cub Scouting's Leave No Trace Awareness Award. (See pages 226 and 227.)

7a Complete the Character Connection for Respect.

Respect

practice

Know. Discuss these questions with your family: What things have people done to show a lack of respect to our world? Why is it important to respect your environment and natural resources? How can you show respect for your environment?

Commit. Discuss with your family how you feel when you see places in your neighborhood that have lots of litter. Name one thing you can do to help the environment.

Practice. Practice being respectful while doing the requirements for "Your Living World."

| Akela's OK | Date | Recorded by the den leader |

7b Land, air, and water can get dirty. Discuss with your family ways this can happen.

| Akela's OK | Date | Recorded by the den leader |

7c It takes a lot of energy to make glass, cans and paper products. You can help save energy by collecting these items for use again. Find out how recycling is done where you live. Find out what items you can recycle.

Recycling bin

RECYCLING

c

Akela's OK   Date   Recorded by the den leader

REQUIREMENT

7d With an adult, pick up litter in your neighborhood. Wear gloves to protect your hands against germs and cuts from sharp objects.

d

Akela's OK   Date   Recorded by the den leader

7e

With an adult, find three stories that tell how people are protecting our world. Read and discuss them together.

| Akela's OK | Date | Recorded by the den leader |

7f

Besides recycling, there are other ways to save energy. List three ways you can save energy, and do them.

1. _____
2. _____
3. _____

Keep the temperature in your home moderate—not too hot in the winter and not too cold in the summer.

Keep the refrigerator door closed.

| Akela's OK | Date | Recorded by the den leader |

8 Cooking and Eating

It's fun to be the cook. The cook fixes the meal and might or might not use a stove. You won't need a stove for most sandwiches and salads.

Study the Food Guide Pyramid. Name some foods from each of the food groups.

8a

Go to www.mypyramid.gov to learn exactly how many servings a day your body needs from each food group.

MyPyramid.gov
STEPS TO A HEALTHIER YOU

Grains—Make half your grains whole. Eat at least 3 ounces of whole-grain cereals, breads, crackers, rice, or pasta every day. (If it's white, it's not whole-grain.) One ounce is about 1 slice of bread, about 1 cup of breakfast cereal, or ½ cup of cooked rice, cereal, or pasta.

Vegetables—Vary your veggies. Eat more dark-green veggies like broccoli, spinach, and other dark leafy greens. Eat more orange vegetables like carrots and sweet potatoes. Eat more dry beans and peas like pinto beans, kidney beans, and lentils.

Fruits—Focus on fruits. Eat a variety of fruit. Choose fresh, frozen, canned, or dried fruit. Examples are apples, strawberries, bananas, peaches, grapes. Go easy on fruit juices (they high in sugar and low in fiber).

Fats, sugars, and salt (sodium)—Choose these with caution. Get most of your fat from fish, nuts, and vegetable oils. Eat less solid fats like butter, stick margarine, shortening, and lard. Check food labels to keep your saturated fats, trans fats, and sodium lower. Choose foods and beverages that are low in added sugar.

Milk—Get your calcium-rich foods. Go low-fat or fat-free when you choose milk, yogurt, and other milk products. If you can't drink milk, choose lactose-free products or foods and beverages with added calcium.

Meat and beans—Go lean with protein. Choose low-fat or lean meats and poultry. Bake it, broil it, or grill it (don't fry it). Vary your protein routine—choose more fish, beans, peas, nuts, and seeds.

Water—Not on the pyramid, but essential. Be sure you drink plenty of water, too, especially if you've been playing hard, hiking, or exercising.

Akela's OK | Date | Recorded by the den leader

8b Plan the meals you and your family should have for one day. List things your family should have from the food groups shown in the Food Guide Pyramid. At each meal, you should have foods from at least three food groups.

Breakfast	Lunch	Dinner
egg	Wrape	rice
blueberry	(chicken)	chicken
toast	Cantolope	veggies
milk		(Carrots)

b

Akela's OK _____ Date _____ Recorded by the den leader

8c Help fix at least one meal for your family. Help set the table, cook the food, and wash the dishes.

Foods, dishes, knives, forks, and spoons must be clean. If they are dirty, you might get sick.

c

Akela's OK _____ Date _____ Recorded by the den leader

REQUIREMENT 8d

Fix your own breakfast. Wash and put away the dishes.

d   Akela's OK _____ Date _____ Recorded by the den leader

REQUIREMENT 8e

With an adult, help to plan, prepare, and cook an outdoor meal.

e   Akela's OK _____ Date _____ Recorded by the den leader

Be Safe at Home and on the Street

You can be careful and safe and still have fun. It's a lot more fun if you and other people don't get hurt. Let's learn how to be safe at home, and outside, too.

Complete the Character Connection for Responsibility.

Responsibility

Know. Discuss these questions with your family: How does being responsible help us be safe? Within the past week, how did you show responsibility?

Commit. Discuss these questions with your family: What happens when people are not responsible? What things can make you forget to be responsible? What things will help you be more responsible?

Practice. Practice being responsible while doing the requirements for "Be Safe at Home and on the Street."

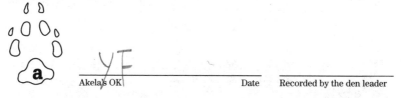

| Akela's OK | Date | Recorded by the den leader |

WITH AN ADULT, check your home for hazards and know how to make your home safe.

Keep tools and toys in their places.

Keep storage areas clear of waste and trash.

Use a step stool and stepladder to reach high places.

Be sure poisons are marked and stored where children can't get them.

Dry your hands before touching an electric switch.

Keep stairs clear. Help put things where they belong in closets, the attic, basement, or storeroom.

Keep closets neat.

Know where the water shutoff valve is.

Know where the electric fuse box or circuit breaker box is.

Know what to do if you smell gas or propane in your home.

Akela's OK	Date	Recorded by the den leader

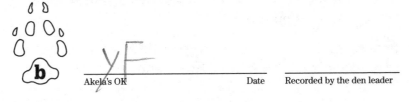

REQUIREMENT 9c   **WITH AN ADULT, check your home for danger from fire.**

Be sure your home has at least one smoke detector. Check the battery.

Plan a family escape route from your home. Draw a floor plan and show the ways your family can get out in case of fire. Know where to meet outside.

Ask an adult to keep gasoline and other dangerous things marked and away from fires or strong heat.

Keep matches where small children cannot reach them. **NEVER PLAY WITH MATCHES!**

Know where the fire exits are in every building you enter. Look for EXIT signs.

Visit a fire station to learn how you can prevent fires.

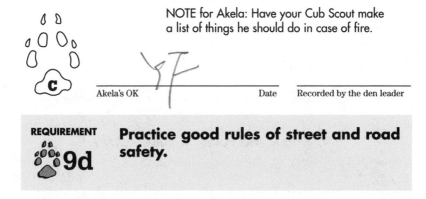

NOTE for Akela: Have your Cub Scout make a list of things he should do in case of fire.

Akela's OK   Date   Recorded by the den leader

REQUIREMENT 9d   **Practice good rules of street and road safety.**

Don't play in the street.

Walk on the left side of the road when there is no sidewalk. Face traffic, watch out for cars.

Obey traffic signs.

Wear your seat belt while riding in a vehicle.

Cross at crosswalks. Watch traffic and look both ways before you step into the street.

Akela's OK   Date   Recorded by the den leader

REQUIREMENT
9e

Know the rules of bike safety.

If you have to ride in the road, keep to the right. Always ride *with* traffic.

Always wear a bicycle helmet.

Ride your bike in a safe place.

Watch out for others.

Don't be a show-off.

Watch out for drain grates.

Check your bike to make sure that everything is working properly.

With your left arm, show others what you are going to do.

Left turn   **Right turn**   **Stop or slow**

Always wear a bicycle helmet.

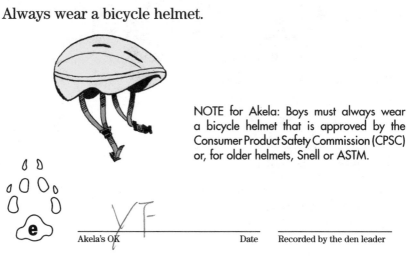

NOTE for Akela: Boys must always wear a bicycle helmet that is approved by the Consumer Product Safety Commission (CPSC) or, for older helmets, Snell or ASTM.

Akela's OK   Date   Recorded by the den leader

Family Fun

Here are some things to do that are fun for everyone. There are games to play, places to go, and things to do with your family.

Do requirement a and do TWO of requirements 10b through 10g.

REQUIREMENT

10a Complete the Character Connection for Cooperation.

Cooperation

practice

Know. Discuss these questions with your family: What is "cooperation"? Why do people need to cooperate when they are doing things together? Name some ways that you can be helpful and cooperate with others.

Commit. Discuss with your family what makes it hard to cooperate. How do listening, sharing, and persuading help us cooperate?

Practice. Practice being cooperative while doing the requirements for "Family Fun."

_____   _____
Akela's OK   Date   Recorded by the den leader

REQUIREMENT

Make a game like one of these. Play it with your family.

Eagle Golf

Take turns dropping beans straight down into a small tin can. Each time a bean goes into the can is 1 point. To win, you must get as many points as you are old before the other players do.

Tin can ⟶

Beanbag Archery

The leader tosses a beanbag out as a target. The other players try to hit it. The closest one becomes the leader for the next toss.

Akela's OK   Date   Recorded by the den leader

REQUIREMENT 10c

Plan a walk. Go to a park or a wooded area, or visit a zoo or museum with your family.

c

Akela's OK _____ Date _____ Recorded by the den leader

REQUIREMENT 10d

Read a book or *Boys' Life* magazine with your family. Take turns reading aloud.

d

Akela's OK _____ Date _____ Recorded by the den leader

10e

Decide with Akela what you will watch on television or listen to on the radio.

Akela's OK   Date   Recorded by the den leader

REQUIREMENT

10f

Attend a concert, a play, or other live program with your family.

Akela's OK   Date   Recorded by the den leader

Have a Family Board Game Night at home with members of your family.

Akela's OK   Date   Recorded by the den leader

11 Duty to God

A Cub Scout promises to do his duty to God. What is your duty to God? How do you do it? Your family can help you learn about God.

11a Complete the Character Connection for Faith.

Faith

Know. What is "faith"? With your family, discuss some people who have shown their faith—who have shown an inner strength based on their trust in a higher power or cause. Discuss the good qualities of these people.

Commit. Discuss these questions with your family: What problems did these faithful people overcome to follow or practice their beliefs? What challenges might you face in doing your duty to God? Who can help you with these challenges?

Practice. Practice your faith while doing the requirements for "Duty to God."

Akela's OK   Date   Recorded by the den leader

Talk with your family about what they believe is their duty to God.

Cub Scout Promise

I, ... ,
promise to do my best
To do my duty to God and
my country,
To help other people, and
To obey the Law of the Pack.

Akela's OK   Date   Recorded by the den leader

Give two ideas on how you can practice or demonstrate your religious beliefs. Choose one and do it.

Akela's OK   Date   Recorded by the den leader

Find out how you can help your church, synagogue, mosque, temple, or religious fellowship.

I found out that I can _____

_____

_____

_____

_____

_____

_____

Akela's OK   Date   Recorded by the den leader

As a Cub Scout, you may earn the religious emblem of your faith. Talk to your religious leader about it.

Metta
Buddhist

Aleph
Jewish

Love for God
Meher Baba

God and Me
Protestant

Bismillah
Islamic

**Unity of
Mankind**
Baha'i

Saint George
Eastern Orthodox

Saint Gregory
Armenian
Churches
(Eastern Diocese)

Joyful Servant
Churches of Christ

God and Country
First Church
of Christ, Scientist
(Christian Science)

Love of God
Polish National
Catholic

Light of Christ
Roman Catholic and
Eastern-Rite Catholic

Dharma
Hindu

That of God
Religious Society
of Friends
(Quakers)

Faith In God
Church of Jesus Christ
of Latter-day Saints
(religious emblems square knot)

**Religious emblems
square knot**

NOTE for Akela: Ask your religious leader or local council service center about the religious emblems programs available to Cub Scouts.

12 Making Choices

We have to make choices all the time. What to do. Where to go. Who to be with. Doing these requirements with an adult family member will help you learn how to make the best choices.

Do requirement a and do FOUR of requirements 12b through 12k.

12a Complete the Character Connection for Courage.

Courage

Know. Discuss with your family what "courage" is? Review the requirements and discuss how you might need courage in each one to do what is right.

Commit. Give some examples of when it is hard to do the right thing. Discuss with your family times that it might take courage to be honest and kind. Tell about a time in your life when you needed to be brave or courageous to do the right thing.

Practice. Practice learning about courage while doing the requirements for "Making Choices." With family members, act out the choices you would make for some of the requirements.

Akela's OK   Date   Recorded by the den leader

There is an older boy who hangs around Jason's school. He tries to give drugs to the children. What would you do if you were Jason?

I would _____

_____

_____

_____

b _____

Akela's OK　　　　　　　　Date　　Recorded by the den leader

Lee is home alone. The phone rings. When Lee answers, a stranger asks whether Lee's mother is home. She is not. Lee is alone. What would you do if you were Lee?

I would Say my mom is busy. She'll
call you back. can you give leave
a message.

_____

c _____

Akela's OK　　　　　　　　Date　　Recorded by the den leader

REQUIREMENT 12d

Justin is new to your school. He has braces on his legs and walks with a limp. Some of the kids at school tease him. They want you to tease him, too. What would you do?

I would _not follow them and I'm going to help him when he needs._

d

Akela's OK   Date   Recorded by the den leader

REQUIREMENT 12e

Juan is on a walk with his little sister. A car stops and a man asks them to come over to the car. What would you do if you were Juan?

I would _walk back to home and tell your parents._

e

Akela's OK   Date   Recorded by the den leader

12f Matthew's grandmother gives him money to buy an ice-cream cone. On the way to the store, a bigger boy asks for money and threatens to hit Matthew if he does not give him some money. If you were Matthew, what would you do?

I would _____

_____

_____

_____

_____

Akela's OK   Date   Recorded by the den leader

REQUIREMENT

12g Chris and his little brother are home alone in the afternoon. A woman knocks on the door and says she wants to read the meter. She is not wearing a uniform. What would you do if you were Chris?

I would _____

_____

_____

_____

_____

Akela's OK   Date   Recorded by the den leader

12h Sam is home alone. He looks out the window and sees a man trying to break into a neighbor's back door. What would you do if you were Sam?

I would Call 911 or call my mom and Dad.

_____

_____

h

Akela's OK YF   Date   Recorded by the den leader

12i Mr. Palmer is blind. He has a guide dog. One day as he is crossing the street, some kids whistle and call to the dog. They want you and your friends to call the dog, too. What would you do?

I would _____

_____

_____

i

Akela's OK   Date   Recorded by the den leader

REQUIREMENT 12j

Some kids who go to Bob's school want him to steal candy and gum from a store, which they can share later. Bob knows this is wrong, but he wants to be popular with these kids. What would you do if you were Bob?

I would _____

_____

_____

Akela's OK   Date   Recorded by the den leader

REQUIREMENT 12k

Paul and his little sister are playing outdoors. A very friendly, elderly woman stops and watches the children for a while. Paul doesn't know the woman. She starts to talk with them and offers to take Paul's little sister on a walk around the block. What would you do?

I would _____

_____

_____

Akela's OK   Date   Recorded by the den leader

When you have filled in 58 of my tracks through all 12 parts of the Wolf trail, you have earned the right to wear my BADGE.

Your Wolf badge will be presented at the pack meeting.

You Are Now a

Wolf Cub Scout.

Arrow Point Trail

NOW, you can earn a

GOLD Arrow Point

and

SILVER Arrow Points.

 This arrow point tells you what to do.

 Fill in this arrow point when you have done it.

With your first 10 filled-in arrow points you can get your

GOLD Arrow Point;

---

10 more gives you a

SILVER Arrow Point;

---

and 10 more gives you another

SILVER Arrow Point;

---

and so on. You can keep track of your arrow points on pages 235 and 236.

It's a Secret

Learn to send secret messages. Only those who know the secret code can read them. Learn to "talk" with your hands.

a Use a secret code.

You can use numbers for letters.

1	A	14	N
2	B	15	O
3	C	16	P
4	D	17	Q
5	E	18	R
6	F	19	S
7	G	20	T
8	H	21	U
9	I	22	V
10	J	23	W
11	K	24	X
12	L	25	Y
13	M	26	Z

13	25	14	1	13	5	9	19	10	9	13	.
M	Y	N	A	M	E	I	S	J	I	M	.

23	8	1	20	9	19	25	15	21	18	19	?
W	H	A	T	I	S	Y	O	U	R	S	?

Or turn the alphabet upside down.

A	Z	N	M
B	Y	O	L
C	X	P	K
D	W	Q	J
E	V	R	I
F	U	S	H
G	T	T	G
H	S	U	F
I	R	V	E
J	Q	W	D
K	P	X	C
L	O	Y	B
M	N	Z	A

R   ZN   VRTSG
I   AM   EIGHT

SLD LOW ZIV BLF?

DSZG RH BLFI OZHG MZNV?

My code is _____

Akela's OK   Date   Recorded by the den leader

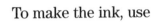
To make the ink, use  milk or lemon juice.

Jim —
Meet me
after school
today —
Pete

Use a toothpick or a small brush for a pen.

When the "ink" dries, you can't see it until you hold it over a light. The heat from the light will turn the "ink" light brown.

b

Akela's OK   Date   Recorded by the den leader

"Write" your name using American Sign Language. People who are deaf use this language.

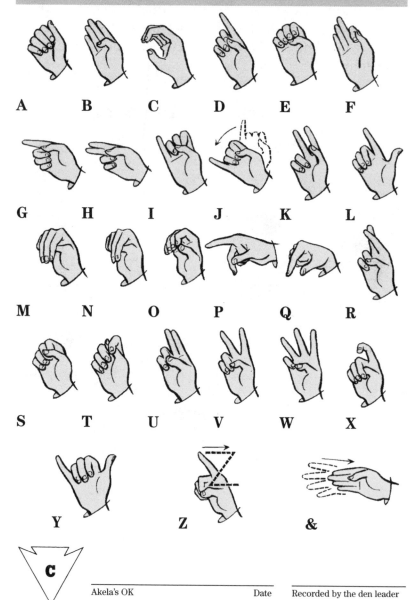

A   B   C   D   E   F

G   H   I   J   K   L

M   N   O   P   Q   R

S   T   U   V   W   X

Y   Z   &

C

| Akela's OK | Date | Recorded by the den leader |

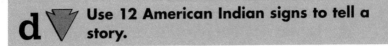

d ▽ **Use 12 American Indian signs to tell a story.**

Sometimes, American Indians would "talk" to others by using a sign language. This way, members of different tribes who didn't share a spoken language could still communicate.

American Indian Sign Language

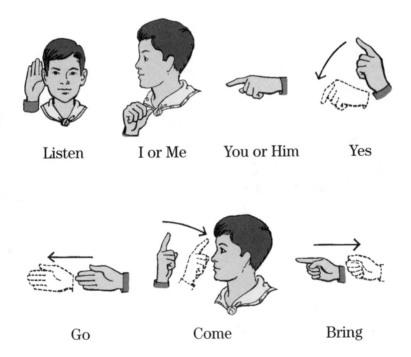

Listen   I or Me   You or Him   Yes

Go   Come   Bring

Walk   Night   Sun   Moon

Hungry   Take   Run

  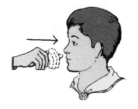

With   Day   Eat

Drink   Sleep   Water

Friend

Talk

Man

Woman

Mind

Scout

Sunrise

Tongue

Heart

Good

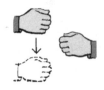

Brave

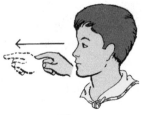

True

What do these say?

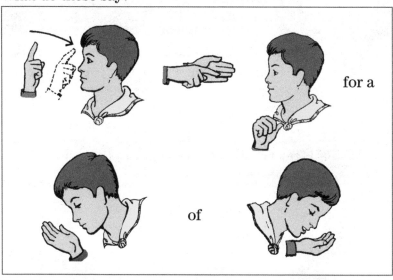

for a

of

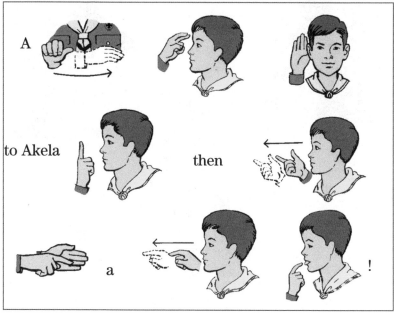

A

to Akela

then

a

!

Be an Actor

It's fun to be an actor. You can make-believe you are anyone you want to be.

a ▽ Help to plan and put on a skit with costumes.

| Akela's OK | Date | Recorded by the den leader |

Make a tepee.

Cover the frame
with paper.

Make a pretend fire.

Tie rolled newspapers
and stack them.

Insert a 15-watt yellow
or red bulb.

Akela's OK	Date	Recorded by the den leader

1. Pound plastic bowls or coconut shells on a board for the clop-clop sound of horses.

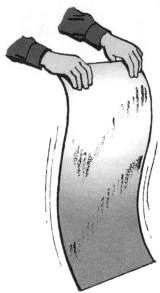

2. Rattle poster board or a metal sheet for thunder.

3. Roll dried peas in a can for rain.

4. Snap a belt or slap the floor or a table for a gunshot.

5. Use a bicycle bell for a telephone ring.

NOTE for Akela: Make these sounds behind a door or a screen so that the audience will think they are real.

Akela's OK   Date   Recorded by the den leader

Akela's OK	Date	Recorded by the den leader

Make It Yourself

Watch carpenters and craftsmen at work. Learn how to handle tools; then pick a project and do it.

 a Make something useful for your home or school. Start with a recipe card holder.

Recipe Card Holder

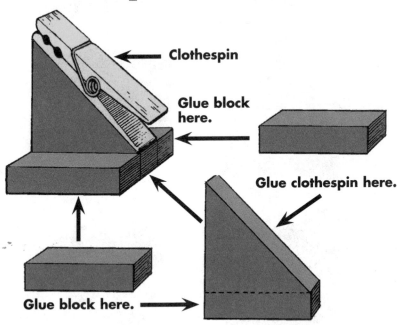

Clothespin

Glue block here.

Glue clothespin here.

Glue block here.

Sand the pieces smooth with sandpaper on a sanding block before you put them together.

Akela's OK   Date   Recorded by the den leader

The ruler on the edge of the page shows measurements in centimeters and in inches. Measure your hand using both kinds of measurements.

This hand span is almost 12 centimeters. How many inches is that?

What's your hand span in centimeters? In inches?

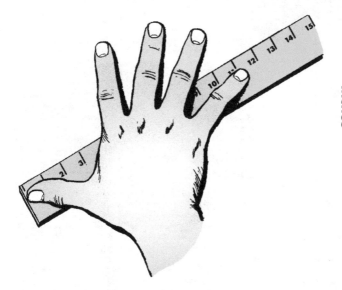

100 centimeters = 1 meter

Meters are used in many sports, such as track and field events.

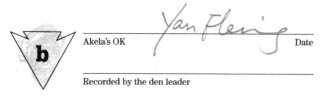

Akela's OK _____ Date

Recorded by the den leader

Inches

Centimeters

Bench Fork

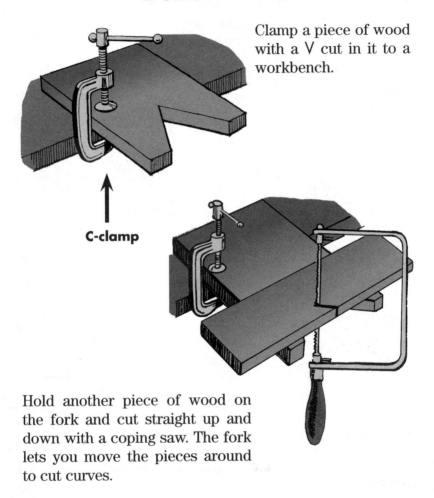

Clamp a piece of wood with a V cut in it to a workbench.

C-clamp

Hold another piece of wood on the fork and cut straight up and down with a coping saw. The fork lets you move the pieces around to cut curves.

Akela's OK	Date	Recorded by the den leader

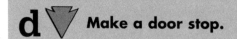
Door Stop

Saw a wedge-shaped piece of wood from the end of a board. Sand it smooth. Paint or stain it.

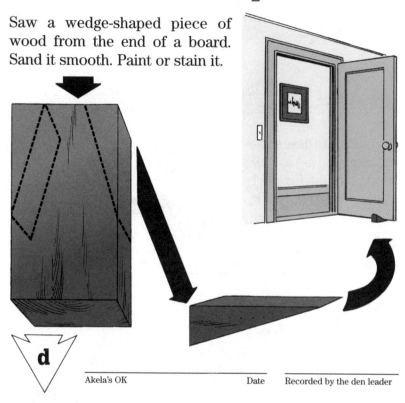

d

Akela's OK | Date | Recorded by the den leader

e Or make something else.

I made a _____

e

Akela's OK | Date | Recorded by the den leader

Elective 3

127

4 Play a Game

Play these games with children younger than you are, with other Cub Scouts, or with grown-ups.

a Play Pie-tin Washer Toss.

Each player tosses five washers at a pie tin. Score 1 point for each washer that stays in the pan.

Akela's OK	Date	Recorded by the den leader

b  Play Marble Sharpshooter.

Each player rolls five marbles at glass bottle targets. Score 1 point for each marble that rolls between the bottles and misses them.

Akela's OK	Date	Recorded by the den leader

C ▽ Play Ring Toss.

Make five rings out of rope, rubber, wire, heavy cardboard, or folded newspaper.

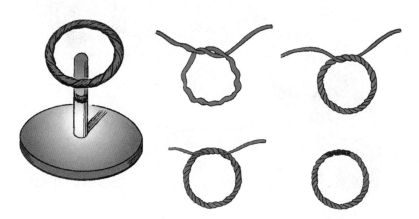

Toss the rings at a stick in the ground or on a stand.

Ringers = 3 points
Leaners = 1 point

_____   _____   _____
Akela's OK   Date   Recorded by the den leader

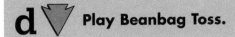

Make a target out of heavy cardboard or a cardboard box. Color it. Each player throws five beanbags. Score 3 points for hitting the eyes, 1 point for the mouth.

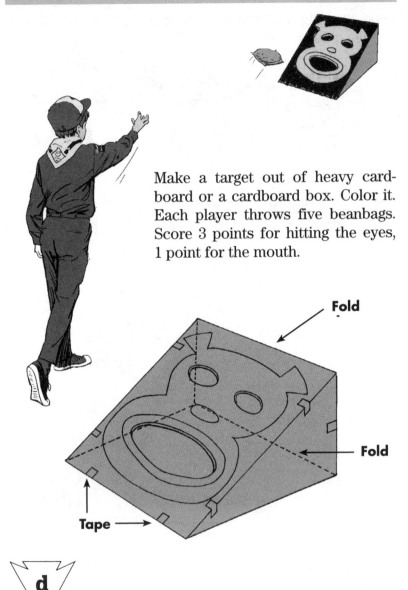

Fold

Fold

Tape →

d

Akela's OK   Date   Recorded by the den leader

e ▽ Play a game of marbles.

Put marbles inside a circle like this.

Stand behind the pitch line and toss your shot toward the lag line.

The player nearest the lag line shoots first from the edge of the circle.

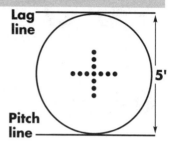

Lag line

5'

Pitch line

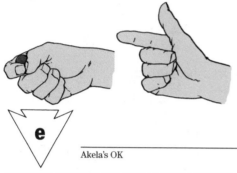

The first player to knock seven marbles out of the circle (with his shooter) is the winner.

e

_____
Akela's OK

_____
Date

_____
Recorded by the den leader

f ▽ Play a wide-area or large group game with your den or pack.

_____
Akela's OK

_____
Date

_____
Recorded by the den leader

Elective 4

Spare-Time Fun

Ride the wind and waves with kites and boats you can make yourself.

a Explain safety rules for kite flying.

 Fly kites away from electrical wires.

 Fly kites in fair weather. Put them away if a storm approaches.

 Make kites with paper and wood, never metal—it might attract lightning.

 Use dry string for kite line.

 Fly kites in an open field or park, never on a street or railroad line.

 If a kite gets caught in wires, a treetop, or somewhere else, have your parent or another adult see if it can be saved.

Remember, have fun but play it safe.

a

Akela's OK   Date   Recorded by the den leader

All you need for a paper-bag kite is a big paper bag and some tape and string.

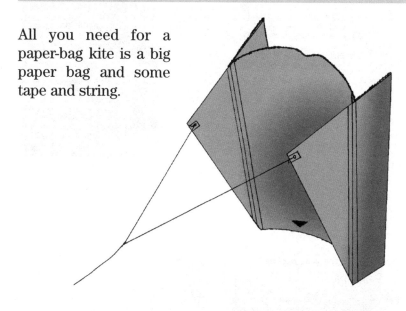

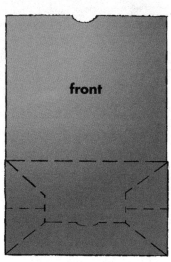

front

1. Cut out the bottom of the bag. Fold down the sides and make the bag flat.

2. Turn the bag over. Make a mark in the center of the bag a third of the way down. Draw lines to the corners and cut out the pieces on this side.

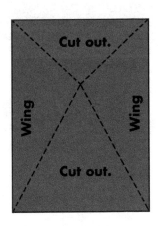

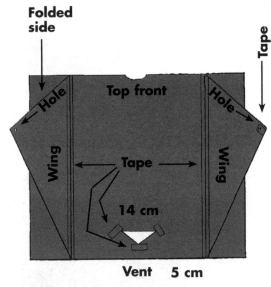

Folded side

Tape

Hole

Top front

Hole

Wing

Tape

Wing

14 cm

Vent   5 cm

Some Cub Scouts tape a tail below the vent.

3. Turn the bag over and tape the wings and folded sides to the front. Tape the ends of the wings. Punch a hole in each wing through the tape for the strings. Cut out a vent near the bottom.

b

Akela's OK   Date   Recorded by the den leader

1.

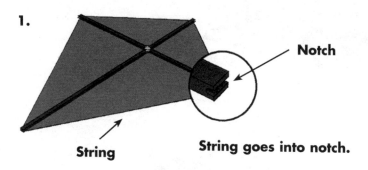

Notch

String

String goes into notch.

2.

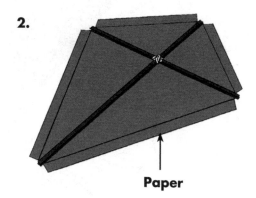

Paper

Fold paper over string and paste.

Bowstring

4.

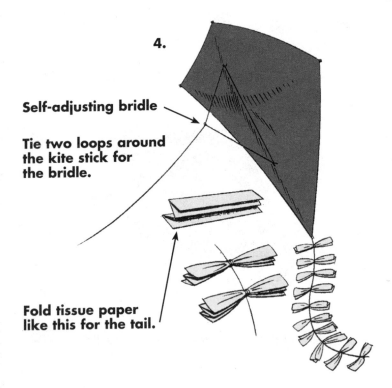

Self-adjusting bridle

Tie two loops around the kite stick for the bridle.

Fold tissue paper like this for the tail.

C

_____   ____   _____
Akela's OK   Date   Recorded by the den leader

x

Arrow Point Trail

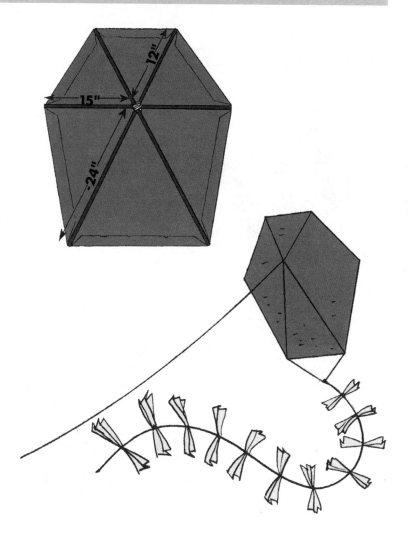

d

_____   _____   _____
Akela's OK   Date   Recorded by the den leader

_____ _____ _____
Akela's OK   Date   Recorded by the den leader

Make two holes in the propeller. Thread the rubber band through one hole and out the other. Attach it to the boat. Wind it up, and let it go!

Wind the propeller this way to make your boat go forward.

Akela's OK   Date   Recorded by the den leader

You can get credit each time you make a different model. You can count the pinewood derby car, raingutter regatta boat, or space derby rocket that you have made.

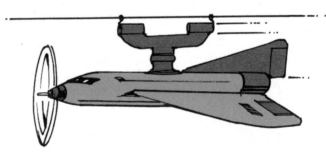

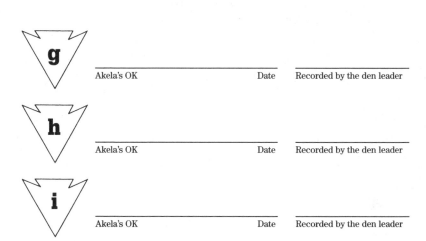

g			
	Akela's OK	Date	Recorded by the den leader

h			
	Akela's OK	Date	Recorded by the den leader

i			
	Akela's OK	Date	Recorded by the den leader

ELECTIVE 6 Books, Books, Books

Books are magical. They are the space-ships of our minds. With them you can go anywhere.

a Visit a bookstore or go to a public library with an adult. Find out how to get your own library card. Name four kinds of books that interest you (for example, history, science fiction, how-to books).

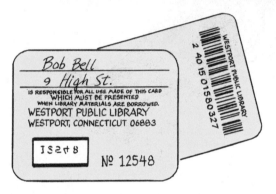

Interesting Books

_____

_____

_____

_____

_____   _____   _____
Akela's OK   Date   Recorded by the den leader

b ▽ Choose a book on a subject you like and read it. With an adult, discuss what you read and what you think about it.

| Akela's OK | Date | Recorded by the den leader |

Books are important. Show that you know how to take care of them. Open a new book the right way. Make a paper or plastic cover for it or another book.

1. Hold the book on a table.

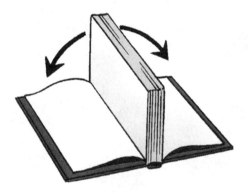

2. Let go of one cover and then the other. Put the covers down gently. Keep the pages closed and upright. Now take a few pages at a time and lightly press them down.

3. Cut paper 3 inches bigger than the book.

4. Fold the top, bottom, and right sides.

5. Slip the book cover into the right-side fold. Make a fold for the front cover. Open the book and slip the front cover into the fold.

Foot Power is a balancing act. Can you walk when your feet are off the ground? It's not as hard as it looks!

a Learn to walk on a pair of stilts.

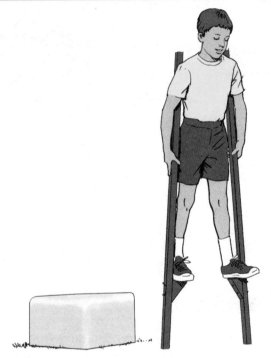

Stand on something to get started.

Akela's OK	Date	Recorded by the den leader

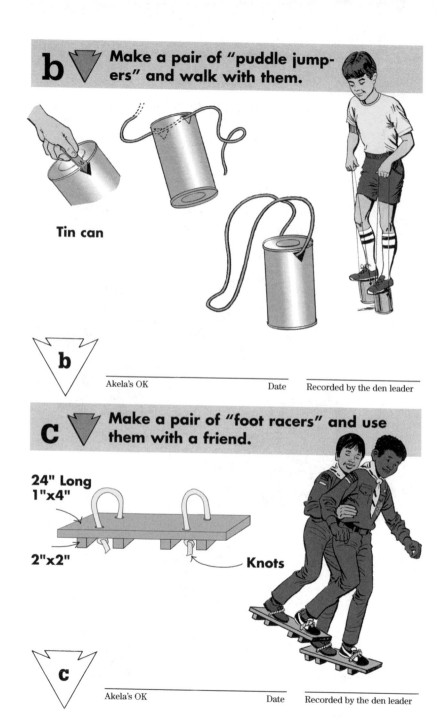

b ▽ Make a pair of "puddle jumpers" and walk with them.

Tin can

c ▽ Make a pair of "foot racers" and use them with a friend.

24" Long
1"x4"

2"x2"

Knots

Elective 7

8 Machine Power

Learn about machines. A stick can be used as a lever. A log can be used as a wheel or a roller. Talk to workers who use levers and wheels every day.

a Name 10 kinds of trucks, construction machinery, or farm machinery and tell what each is used for.

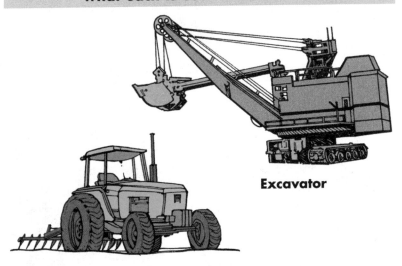

Excavator

Tractor

Cement mixer

Long-haul truck

Dump truck

Tanker truck

NOTE for Akela: Encourage your Cub Scout to find pictures of machinery in newspapers and magazines. He can cut them out and paste them on these pages.

a

Akela's OK   Date   Recorded by the den leader

b ▽ Help an adult do a job using a wheel and axle.

Any cart has wheels and axles.

Most of the load is on the axle. You can move it on the wheel.

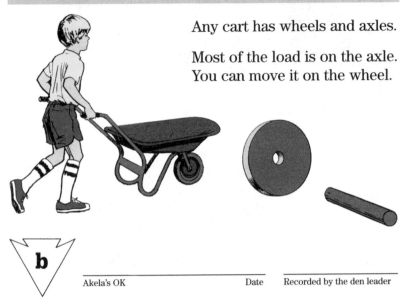

Akela's OK	Date	Recorded by the den leader

c ▽ Show how to use a pulley.

← **Pull this way.**

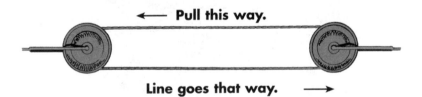

Line goes that way. ⟶

I used a pulley to _____.

Akela's OK	Date	Recorded by the den leader

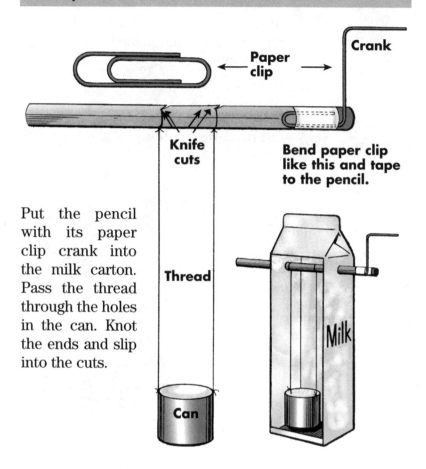

Paper clip

Crank

Knife cuts

Bend paper clip like this and tape to the pencil.

Thread

Put the pencil with its paper clip crank into the milk carton. Pass the thread through the holes in the can. Knot the ends and slip into the cuts.

Can

Milk

Cut one side from a milk carton. Punch holes for the pencil.

d

Let's Have a Party

Parties are more fun when you've made a gift yourself and helped plan and put on the party.

a Help with a home or den party.

Help decorate the room.

Help plan and play games.

Help serve refreshments.

Help clean up afterward.

Talk over your party with Akela. Did your party go as you planned? What did you like about your party? What would you do different for your next party?

| Akela's OK | Date | Recorded by the den leader |

For a beanbag, use scrap cloth or an old pocket. Fill it with dried beans. Fold in the top and sew it shut.

A tin-can pencil holder can be covered with string or paper that is glued to the can.

NOTE for Akela: Boys can give this gift to a friend, a family member, or anyone in a hospital or retirement home. Elective credit may be given for each gift made.

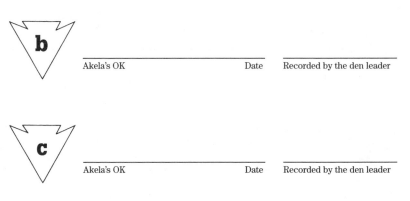

b

_____   _____   _____
Akela's OK   Date   Recorded by the den leader

c

_____   _____   _____
Akela's OK   Date   Recorded by the den leader

American Indian Lore

The first Americans were called Indians because Columbus thought he was near India when he got here. The more you know about these native Americans, the more you will know about America.

a **Read a book or tell a story about American Indians, past or present.**

Pueblo

I read or told a story about_____

_____

_____

_____

Akela's OK	Date	Recorded by the den leader

b ▽ Make a musical instrument American Indians used.

Chamois or vinyl

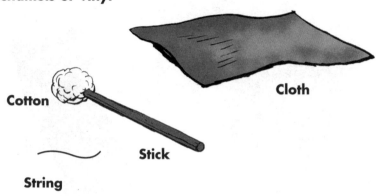

Cloth

Cotton

Stick

String

A big can or something round and hollow

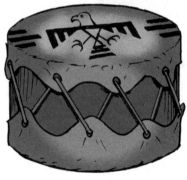

C Make traditional American Indian clothing.

Woodland vest

Plains breechcloth

Northwest Coast hat

Pueblo belt

C

Akela's OK	Date	Recorded by the den leader

d ▽ **Make a traditional item or instrument that American Indians used to make their lives easier.**

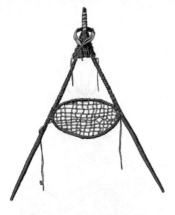

Plains dog travois

Plains parfleche (bag or case)

Plateau snowshoe

Piman carrying basket

Make a model of a traditional American Indian house.

Florida stilt house

California tepee-shaped dwelling

Northwest Coast plank house

Southwestern wickiup

| Akela's OK | Date | Recorded by the den leader |

Big voice

Bear alive

Bear dead

Bad

Top man

Camp

Brothers

Make peace

Council

Talk

Wise man

Hunt

Morning **Noon** **Evening** **Directions**

Man **Woman** **Boy** **Man on horse**

Tepee **Hear** **Spirit** **Birds**

Eat **Deer** **Beaver** **Horses**

| River | Lake | Three Days | Three Nights | Hungry |

| Fear | Look | Campfire | Food |

| Stormy | Clear | Rain | Cold, snow |

f

Akela's OK   Date   Recorded by the den leader

Learn to sing lots of songs. There are glad songs and sad songs, and some are proud, like "The Star-Spangled Banner."

a **Learn and sing the first and last verses of "America."**

America

My country, 'tis of thee,
Sweet land of liberty,
Of thee I sing.
Land where my fathers died!
Land of the Pilgrims' pride!
From ev'ry mountainside,
Let freedom ring!

Our fathers' God, to Thee,
Author of liberty,
To Thee we sing.
Long may our land be bright
With freedom's holy light;
Protect us by Thy might,
Great God, our King!

a

Akela's OK   Date   Recorded by the den leader

The Star-Spangled Banner

Oh, say can you see
　by the dawn's early light
What so proudly we hailed
　at the twilight's last gleaming?
Whose broad stripes and bright stars
　through the perilous fight,
O'er the ramparts we watched
　were so gallantly streaming?
And the rocket's red glare,
　the bombs bursting in air,
Gave proof through the night
　that our flag was still there.
Oh, say does that star-spangled
　banner yet wave
O'er the land of the free
　and the home of the brave?

Akela's OK　　　　　　　Date　　Recorded by the den leader

You can find other songs in the *Cub Scout Songbook.*

Good Night, Cub Scouts

(Tune: "Good Night, Ladies")

Good night, Cub Scouts.
Good night, Cub Scouts.
Good night, Cub Scouts,
We're going to leave you now.

Merrily we Cub along, Cub along, Cub along.
Merrily we Cub along up the Cub Scout trail.

Sweet dreams, Cub Scouts.
Sweet dreams, Cub Scouts.
Sweet dreams, Cub Scouts,
We're going to leave you now.

I've Got That Cub Scout Spirit

I've got that Cub Scout spirit
Up in my head, up in my head, up in
my head;
I've got that Cub Scout spirit
Up in my head, up in my head to
stay.

*Replace "up in my head" with other words
in the other four verses:*
Second verse: Deep in my heart
Third verse: Down in my feet

Fourth verse: All over me
Fifth verse:
> I've got that Cub Scout spirit
> Up in my head, deep in my heart, down in my feet;
> I've got that Cub Scout spirit
> All over me, all over me to stay.

Train Song

(Tune: "Yankee Doodle")

I met an engine on a hill
All hot and broken-hearted,
And this is what he said to me
As up the hill he started.

(Slowly)

I think I can, I think I can,
At any rate, I'll try.
I think I can, I think I can,
At any rate, I'll try.

He reached the top, and looking back
To where he stood and doubted,
He started on the downward track
And this is what he shouted:

(Faster)

I knew I could, I knew I could,
I never should have doubted.
I knew I could, I knew I could,
I never should have doubted!

Akela's OK   Date   Recorded by the den leader

d ▽ Learn the words and sing the first verse of three other songs, hymns, or prayers. Write the verse of one of the songs you learned in the space below.

▽ **d**

_____ _____ _____
Akela's OK   Date   Recorded by the den leader

e ▽ Learn and sing a song that would be sung as a grace before meals. Write the words in the space below.

▽ **e**

_____ _____ _____
Akela's OK   Date   Recorded by the den leader

Akela's OK	Date	Recorded by the den leader

Be an Artist

You can't tell if you can draw a picture until you try. Someday, you could become an artist or a drafter.

a ▽ **Make a freehand sketch of a person, place, or thing.**

Draw here or on a piece of paper.

Akela's OK   Date   Recorded by the den leader

C Mix yellow and blue paints, mix yellow and red, and mix red and blue. Tell what color you get from each mixture.

Color wheel

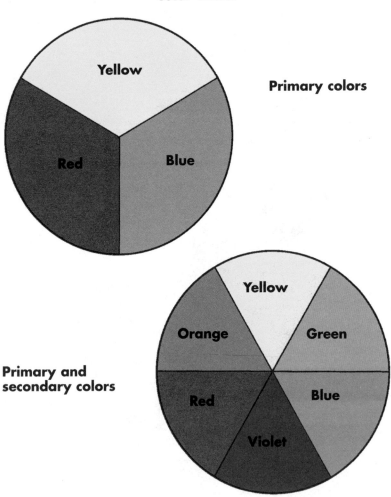

Primary colors

Primary and secondary colors

Color wheel labels: Yellow, Red, Blue

Second wheel labels: Yellow, Orange, Green, Red, Blue, Violet

C

Akela's OK _____ Date _____ Recorded by the den leader

Help draw, paint, or color some scenery for a skit, play, or puppet show.

Use a large sheet of paper or cardboard.

City

Country

Akela's OK   Date   Recorded by the den leader

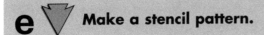
Draw.

Cut out.

Use heavy paper. Cut
out the parts that will be
painted. Place them on a
sheet of paper and paint.

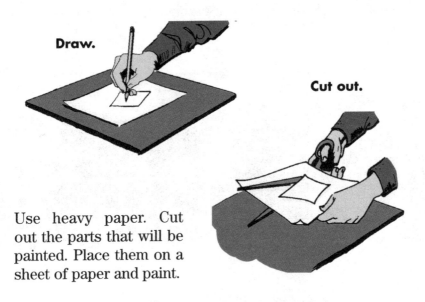

Paint.

Akela's OK	Date	Recorded by the den leader

f **Make a poster for a Cub Scout project or a pack meeting.**

ELECTIVE 13 Birds

Some birds are summer visitors. Others pass through in the spring and fall, while still others live in the same area all year. They all need homes and food.

This elective is also part of the Cub Scout World Conservation Award. (See page 226.)

 Make a list of all the birds you saw in a week and tell where you saw them (field, forest, marsh, yard, or park).

| Robin | Sparrow | Goose | Seagull |

| Duck | Goldfinch | Blue jay | Cardinal |

Akela's OK   Date   Recorded by the den leader

b Put out nesting material (short pieces of yarn and string) for birds and tell which birds might use it.

b

_____   _____
Akela's OK   Date   Recorded by the den leader

c Read a book about birds.

I read _____

c

_____   _____
Akela's OK   Date   Recorded by the den leader

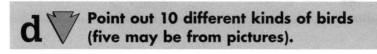

d Point out 10 different kinds of birds (five may be from pictures).

d

_____   _____
Akela's OK   Date   Recorded by the den leader

Feed wild birds and tell which birds you fed.

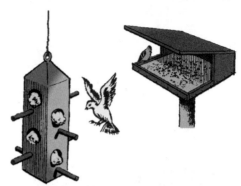

Birds like bread crumbs, cracked corn, sunflower seeds, millet, or other grains.

Make your own birdbath.

Keep the birdbath clean.

Garbage can top

Two-by-fours

Piece of broomstick

Akela's OK _____ Date _____ Recorded by the den leader

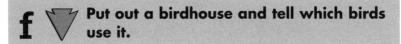

Lift the top to clean out the birdhouse.

Clean the birdhouse each year in the fall.

Akela's OK   Date   Recorded by the den leader

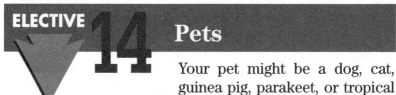

ELECTIVE 14 Pets

Your pet might be a dog, cat, guinea pig, parakeet, or tropical fish. All pets need care—even crickets.

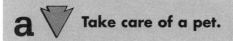

a ▽ **Take care of a pet.**

Dogs need a clean place to live. Give your dog water and dog food. Don't feed your dog small bones.

Feed your bird birdseed, grit, and water.

Keep the cage clean.

Gerbils, hamsters, guinea pigs, white mice, and rats need prepared food, nuts, seeds, and water. Clean the cage every day.

Cats are good companions. Give them cat food, not table scraps, which contain too much fat and starch. Always keep fresh water available.

Feed fish prepared fish food. Keep the fish bowl or aquarium clean.

My pet is a _____.

Its name is _____.

Akela's OK	Date	Recorded by the den leader

b ▽ Know what to do when you meet a strange dog.

Do not go up to a strange dog. If a dog comes up to you

1. Stand up straight with your hands down. Let the dog sniff the back of your hand.

2. Don't make any quick moves and don't pet the dog.

3. Don't try to scare the dog away or show that you are afraid.

4. Wait until the dog leaves, then walk away quietly. Don't run.

Akela's OK   Date   Recorded by the den leader

I read _____.

d Tell what is meant by *rabid.* Name some animals that can have rabies. Tell what you should do if you see a dog or wild animal that is behaving strangely. Tell what you should do if you find a dead animal.

Raccoons, skunks, foxes, and bats can have rabies.

Rabid means **SICK!**

Don't go near wild animals that seem to be **TAME.**

Don't go near a dog that seems to be

CHOKING

EXCITED

AFRAID

Don't touch a dead animal.

Tell an adult right away if you are bitten or scratched by any pet or wild animal, or if you find one that is sick or dead.

d

Akela's OK   Date   Recorded by the den leader

Grow Something

Growing a garden is almost like magic. You put tiny seeds into the ground, and presto, little green plants spring up.

This elective is also part of the Cub Scout World Conservation Award. (See page 226.)

 a Plant and raise a box garden.

Put stones in the bottom and soil on the top. Pour water into the pipe.

I grew _____ .

Akela's OK	Date	Recorded by the den leader

b ▽ **Plant and raise a flower bed.**

I grew _____.

_____   _____   _____
Akela's OK   Date   Recorded by the den leader

Pineapple **Grapefruit** **Mimosa** **Avocado** **Sweet potato**

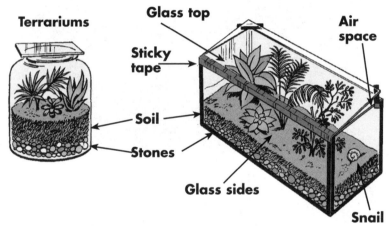

Terrariums **Glass top** **Air space**

Sticky tape

Soil

Stones

Glass sides

Snail

I grew _____ .

NOTE for Akela: Ivy, moss, and lichens will grow in a glass-covered terrarium that holds heat and moisture.

C

Akela's OK   Date   Recorded by the den leader

d ▽ Plant and raise vegetables.

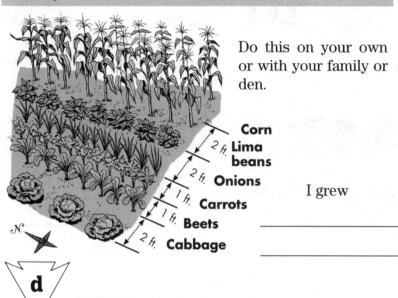

Do this on your own or with your family or den.

Corn
2 ft. Lima beans
2 ft. Onions
1 ft. Carrots
1 ft. Beets
2 ft. Cabbage

I grew

_____

_____

▽ **d**

_____   _____
Akela's OK   Date   Recorded by the den leader

e ▽ Visit a botanical garden or other agricultural exhibition in your area.

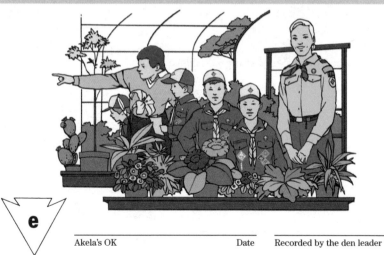

▽ **e**

_____   _____
Akela's OK   Date   Recorded by the den leader

Elective 15   **187**

ELECTIVE 16 — Family Alert

Would you know what to do if your home were hit by a tornado, flood, or hurricane? Here are three things you can do.

a ▽ **Talk with your family about what you will do in an emergency.**

In case of a fire or other emergency we will _____

_____

_____.

My job is to _____

_____

_____.

NOTE to Akela: Guide your Cub Scout in this project, depending upon your own home, needs, and types of emergencies in your area.

| Akela's OK | Date | Recorded by the den leader |

b ▽ In case of a bad storm or flood, know where you can get safe food and water in your home. Tell how to purify water. Show one way. Know where and how to shut off water, electricity, gas, or oil.

I purified water by——————————————————

_____

_____.

We have emergency food and clothing in the _____

_____.

NOTE for Akela: Boil water for 5 minutes. Ask a health officer for other methods. Tell your Cub Scout where he can get safe food and water in an emergency.

▽**b**

_____   _____   _____
Akela's OK   Date   Recorded by the den leader

C ▽ Make a list of your first-aid supplies, or make a first-aid kit. Know where the first-aid things are kept.

▽**c**

_____   _____   _____
Akela's OK   Date   Recorded by the den leader

Tie It Right

Do your shoes come untied all by themselves? Maybe the knots you tie are to blame.

 a Learn to tie an overhand knot and a square knot.

Overhand knot

Square knot

A square knot begins with an overhand knot and ends with another one backwards on top of the first.

Akela's OK	Date	Recorded by the den leader

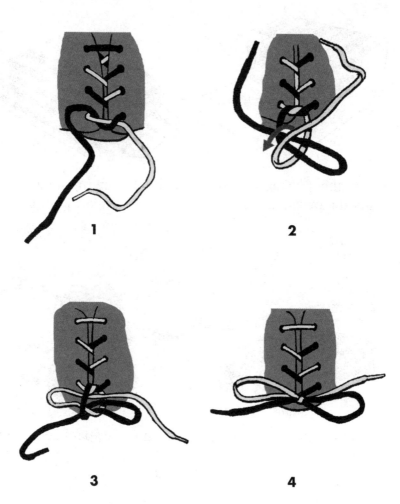

1

2

3

4

b

Akela's OK   Date   Recorded by the den leader

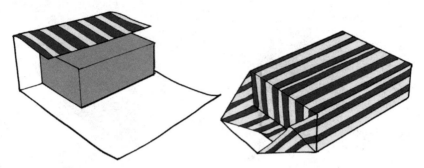
1. Put the package in the middle of the paper.

2. Fold over the long sides of the paper. Fold in the ends.

3. Take the string or ribbon once around and then cross over.

4. Flip the package over and tie with a square knot.

| Akela's OK | Date | Recorded by the den leader |

d ▽ Tie a stack of newspapers the right way.

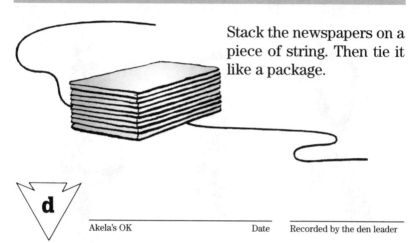

Stack the newspapers on a piece of string. Then tie it like a package.

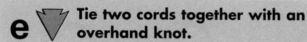

d

Akela's OK   Date   Recorded by the den leader

e ▽ Tie two cords together with an overhand knot.

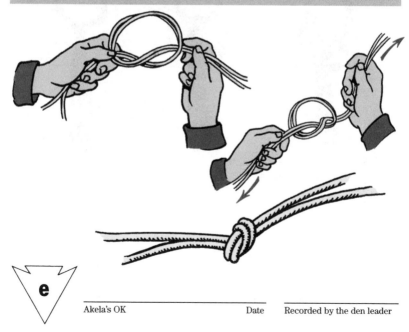

e

Akela's OK   Date   Recorded by the den leader

1

2

3

4

5

6

Akela's OK	Date	Recorded by the den leader

This is called "whipping" the rope.

Twisted rope

Braided rope

Akela's OK	Date	Recorded by the den leader

Outdoor Adventure

A lot of Cub Scouting belongs outdoors with picnics, treasure hunts, and adventure trails.

NOTE for Akela: Follow these sun safety rules from the American Academy of Dermatology: (1) Stay out of the sun between 10 A.M. and 4 P.M. when the sun's rays are the strongest. (2) Use sunscreen with a sun protection factor (SPF) of at least 15; put on more every two hours, even on cloudy days. (3) Wear protective, tightly woven clothing, such as a long-sleeved shirt and pants. (4) Wear a 4-inch-wide broad-brimmed hat and sunglasses with UV protective lenses. (5) Stay in the shade whenever you can. (6) Stay away from reflective surfaces.

 a **Help plan and hold a picnic with your family or den.**

 a

—————————————   —————————————
Akela's OK   Date   Recorded by the den leader

b **With an adult, help plan and run a family or den outing.**

 b

—————————————   —————————————
Akela's OK   Date   Recorded by the den leader

Help plan and lay out a treasure hunt something like this.

I hid my treasure_____

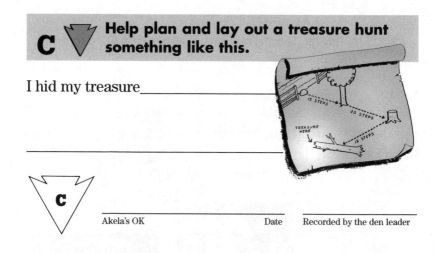

_____

Akela's OK   Date   Recorded by the den leader

d

Help plan and lay out an obstacle race. Use this idea or make up your own.

- Jump across an imaginary river.
- Crawl through a cardboard tunnel.
- Jump up and ring a bell.
- Toss a ball into a can.
- Do one forward roll.
- Walk like an elephant for five steps.

This is what I did:_____

_____

_____

d

Akela's OK   Date   Recorded by the den leader

Help plan and lay out an adventure trail.

In a park or playground, set up five games scattered around the park. Here are five examples:

1 Guess how many beans are in a jar.

2 List as many insects as you can find in 2 minutes.

3 Fold the U.S. flag and read the OUTDOOR CODE:
As an American,
I will do my best to—
Be clean in my outdoor manners,
Be careful with fire,
Be considerate in the outdoors, and
Be conservation minded.

4 Tie your shoes with your eyes shut.

5 Look for colors; listen for sounds.

Akela's OK   Date   Recorded by the den leader

f ▽ **Take part in two summertime pack events with your den.**

I took part in _____ and

_____.

▽ **f**

_____   _____
Akela's OK   Date   Recorded by the den leader

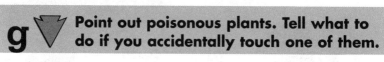

g ▽ **Point out poisonous plants. Tell what to do if you accidentally touch one of them.**

Poison ivy   **Poison sumac**   **Poison oak**

If you touch these plants, wash with soap and cold water. You can also buy special outdoor skin cleansers at the store that work better than soap and water.

▽ **g**

_____   _____
Akela's OK   Date   Recorded by the den leader

When fishing, boys and grown-ups are equal. The fish does not know how old the person is at the other end of the line.

This elective is also part of the Cub Scout World Conservation Award. (See page 226.)

a **Identify five different kinds of fish.**

Here are some you might see:

Perch

Bluegill

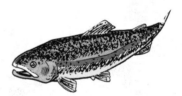

Rainbow trout

Largemouth bass

Catfish

a

_____   _____   _____
Akela's OK   Date   Recorded by the den leader

b ▽ Rig a pole with the right kind of line and hook. Attach a bobber and sinker, if you need them. Then go fishing.

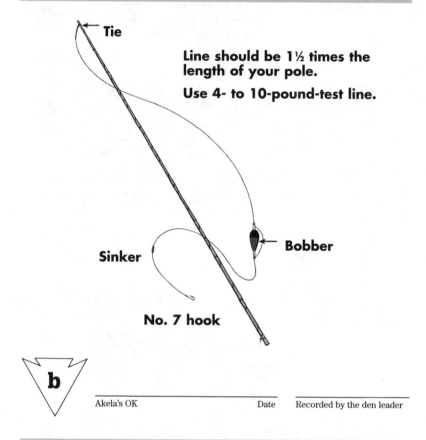

← Tie

Line should be 1½ times the length of your pole.

Use 4- to 10-pound-test line.

Bobber

Sinker

No. 7 hook

 b

_____   _____
Akela's OK   Date   Recorded by the den leader

c ▽ Fish with members of your family or an adult. Bait your hook and do your best to catch a fish.

I caught a _____

▽ **c**

_____   _____
Akela's OK   Date   Recorded by the den leader

Know the rules of safe fishing.

Don't fish here. The bank could cave in.

Watch out for holes and drop-offs.

Be careful of slippery logs and rocks.

That fishhook can catch more than fish. Be careful around other people.

 d

Akela's OK — Date — Recorded by the den leader

 Tell about some of the fishing laws where you live.

 e

Akela's OK — Date — Recorded by the den leader

f ▽ Show how to use a rod and reel.

1. Hold the line with your finger.

2. Cast the rod forward; let up on the line with your finger. When the bait or lure is where you want it, stop the reel by pressing on its edge with a finger.

3. Be sure you have plenty of room.

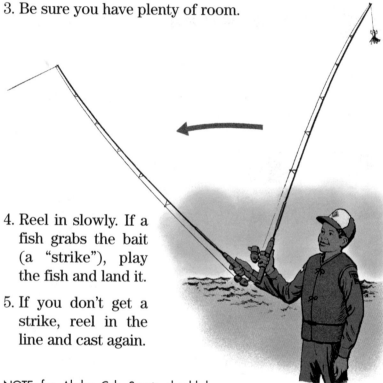

4. Reel in slowly. If a fish grabs the bait (a "strike"), play the fish and land it.

5. If you don't get a strike, reel in the line and cast again.

NOTE for Akela: Cub Scouts should have proper instruction in using rods and reels. Point out safety measures. Adults should go fishing with them.

_____
Akela's OK   Date   Recorded by the den leader

Sports

Before beginning this elective, discuss sportsmanship* with Akela or another adult.

 a **Play a game of tennis, table tennis, or badminton.**

NOTE for Akela: Find someone who knows the game to help you. Also see the badminton, tennis, and table tennis sections in the *Cub Scout Academics and Sports Program Guide.*

a

_____   _____
Akela's OK   Date   Recorded by the den leader

_____

*See discussion in the *Cub Scout Academics and Sports Program Guide.*

b ▽ Know boating safety rules.

1. Go boating only with a grown-up.

2. Wear a personal flotation device.

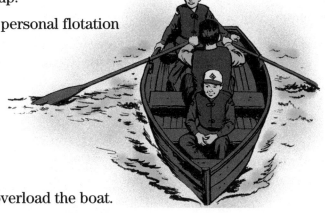

3. Don't overload the boat.

4. Stay with the boat even if it leaks. It will keep you afloat.

5. When you see lightning or a storm coming, head for shore.

NOTE for Akela: Both Safety Afloat and Safe Swim Defense are available through your local council service center.

Akela's OK	Date	Recorded by the den leader

Archery Safety Rules

- Shoot only when a grown-up is with you.

- When handling a bow with an arrow in it (when the arrow is *nocked*), always point the arrow in a safe direction.

- *Nock* the arrow only when told.

- Nock the arrow only when on the firing line.

- Always point the arrow down-range toward the target.

- When not shooting, always point the arrow downward.

- Never shoot straight up in the air.

- Never shoot toward anything other than the target.

- Never shoot a bow without an arrow. You could break the bow.

NOTE for Akela: Archery can be done only at a district or council day camp, resident camp, or family camp.

C

_____   _____   _____
Akela's OK   Date   Recorded by the den leader

d Understand the safety and courtesy code for skiing. Show walking and the kick turn. Do climbing with a side step or herringbone. Show the snowplow or stem turn, and how to get up from a fall.

Skier's Safety and Courtesy Code

- Good skiers always ski under control. This means you must be able to turn and stop at will so that you can avoid running into trees and other skiers.

- Make sure your ski binding holds your foot firmly to your ski and that your release works properly.

- Ski properly clothed and only when weather and conditions permit.

- Wear a ski or winter helmet to protect your head.

- Ski in an area that matches your abilities.

- Respect the rights of other skiers.

- Keep yourself physically fit.

- When skiing downhill and overtaking another skier, stay clear of the other person. Prevent collisions.

- When you and another skier are headed toward each other always stay to the right.

- Do not stop in the middle of a trail. If you fall or must stop, get off to the side of the trail. If your fall left a hole, or *sitzmark*, fill it with loose snow.

- When entering a trail from the side, look up the trail to make sure no skier is coming down. The same holds true when you stop. Check up the slope before you continue to ski down the mountain.

- Never walk on ski trails without skis on your feet.

- Your skis should be equipped with a safety strap or spring-type prongs that grab into the snow when released.

- Read and obey all traffic signs on the ski slopes.

- When using a ski lift, do not cut into the line. Wait your turn.

NOTE for Akela: Find a skier who can help you. Also see the snow ski and board sports section in the *Cub Scout Academics and Sports Program Guide.*

d

_____
Akela's OK   Date   Recorded by the den leader

e Know the safety rules for ice skating. Skate, without falling, as far as you can walk in 50 steps. Come to a stop. Turn from forward to backward.

Ice-Skating Safety Rules

Wear warm clothes!

- Always use sharp skates.
- Skate only on safe ice in places where skating is supervised.
- Never skate alone.
- Never skate or walk on thin ice.
- Never throw anything onto the ice.
- Never push or grab another skater.

NOTE for Akela: Find a skater who can help you. Also see the ice skating section in the *Cub Scout Academics and Sports Program Guide.*

e

Akela's OK   Date   Recorded by the den leader

f ▽ In roller skating, know the safety rules. From a standing start, skate forward as far as you can walk in 50 steps. Come to a stop within 10 walking steps. Skate around a corner one way without coasting. Then do the same coming back. Turn from forward to backward.

Indoor Skating Rules

- Fast skating is not allowed.

- When entering the skating floor, give the right-of-way to other skaters.

- In leaving, move slowly to your right. Don't cut across the path of other skaters.

- Do not push or play games that bother other skaters.

- Skate only in the direction of the skating traffic.

NOTE for Akela: Find a skater who can help you. Also see the roller skating section in the *Cub Scout Academics and Sports Program Guide*.

Outdoor Skating Rules

- On sidewalks, give walkers the right-of-way.
- Don't race out of driveways or alleys.
- Avoid skating on rough pavement.
- Don't skate on other people's property without permission.
- Stop and look both ways before you cross a street.
- Obey traffic laws, signs, and signals.
- Don't skate in the street in traffic.
- Avoid uncontrolled coasting down hills.
- Don't hitch onto bicycles, cars, or trucks.
- Don't skate at night.
- Check your equipment before skating. Be sure all fittings are tight.
- Wear a helmet, gloves, wrist guards, and pads.

NOTE for Akela: ASTM standard or Snell-approved helmet; padded gloves; wrist supports; and elbow, knee, and hip pads should be worn for skating.

f

_____   _____
Akela's OK   Date   Recorded by the den leader

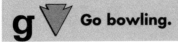
Bowling Basics

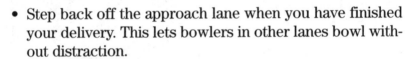

- Wear bowling shoes.

- Choose one bowling ball and use it.

- Bowl when it's your turn.

- Stay in your approach lane.

- Step back off the approach lane when you have finished your delivery. This lets bowlers in other lanes bowl without distraction.

- Pick up the ball with both hands, one on either side of the ball, to avoid pinched fingers and hands.

- Keep the ball on the ball return where it won't roll off and hurt someone.

- Check shoelaces and be sure they are tied.

- Return the bowling ball to the storage rack and rental shoes to the counter.

NOTE for Akela: See the bowling section in the *Cub Scout Academics and Sports Program Guide.*

Akela's OK	Date	Recorded by the den leader

h ▽ **Show how to make a sprint start in track. See how far you can run in 10 seconds.**

(The runs in the Olympic Games are measured in meters. A meter is equal to 39.37 inches.)

Akela's OK	Date	Recorded by the den leader

i ▽ **Do a standing long jump. Jump as far as you can.**

Akela's OK	Date	Recorded by the den leader

j Play a game of flag football.

NOTE for Akela: See the flag football section in the *Cub Scout Academics and Sports Program Guide.*

_____   _____
Akela's OK   Date   Recorded by the den leader

k Show how to dribble and kick a soccer ball. Take part in a game.

NOTE for Akela: See the soccer section in the *Cub Scout Academics and Sports Program Guide.*

_____   _____
Akela's OK   Date   Recorded by the den leader

1 ▽ Play a game of baseball or softball.

NOTE for Akela: See the softball and baseball sections in the *Cub Scout Academics and Sports Program Guide.*

Akela's OK   Date   Recorded by the den leader

m ▽ Show how to shoot, pass, and dribble a basketball. Take part in a game.

NOTE for Akela: See the basketball section in the *Cub Scout Academics and Sports Program Guide.*

Akela's OK   Date   Recorded by the den leader

n ▽ Earn the Cub Scouting shooting sports BB-gun shooting belt loop.

NOTE for Akela: BB-gun shooting can be done only at a district or council day camp, resident camp, council-organized family camp, or a council activity where all standards for BSA shooting sports are enforced.

Akela's OK   Date   Recorded by the den leader

o ▽ With your den, participate in four outdoor physical fitness–related activities.

Akela's OK   Date   Recorded by the den leader

Computers

Computers can make jobs or learning new things easier, and computer games can be fun.

a ▼ **Visit a business where computers are used. Find out what the computers do.**

I visited_____.

_____ _____
Akela's OK   Date   Recorded by the den leader

b Explain what a computer program does. Use a program to write a report for school, to write a letter, or for something

b

Akela's OK   Date   Recorded by the den leader

c Tell what a computer mouse is. Describe how a CD-ROM is used.

c

Akela's OK   Date   Recorded by the den leader

Say It Right

Being able to say what you mean is very important.

a ▽ **Say "hello" in a language other than English.**

FRENCH	GERMAN	HEBREW	ITALIAN
allô	*hallo*	*shalom*	*buon giorno*

SPANISH	SWAHILI	SWEDISH	MANDARIN
hola	*jambo*	*hej*	*Ni hao*

I counted in this language:_____.

Akela's OK   Date   Recorded by the den leader

b ⧨ Count to 10 in a language other than English.

	FRENCH	GERMAN	ITALIAN	SPANISH
1	un	eins	uno	uno
2	deux	zwei	due	dos
3	trois	drei	tre	tres
4	quatre	vier	quattro	cuatro
5	cinq	fünf	cinque	cinco
6	six	sechs	sei	seis
7	sept	sieben	sette	siete
8	huit	acht	otto	ocho
9	neuf	neun	nove	nueve
10	dix	zehn	dieci	diez

NOTE for Akela: Boys may learn to count in a language not listed on the chart.

Language learned:_____.

⧨ **b**

_____   _____

Akela's OK   Date   Recorded by the den leader

Get story ideas from *Boys' Life* and other magazines.

I told a story about _____.

Akela's OK	Date	Recorded by the den leader

d Tell how to get to a nearby fire station or police station from your home, your den meeting place, and school. Use directions and street names.

I gave directions from my house to _____ .

I gave directions from my den meeting place to_____ .

I gave directions from my school to_____ .

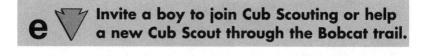

d _____   _____

Akela's OK   Date   Recorded by the den leader

e Invite a boy to join Cub Scouting or help a new Cub Scout through the Bobcat trail.

I invited _____ .

e _____   _____

Akela's OK   Date   Recorded by the den leader

Let's Go Camping!

a ▽ **Participate with your pack on an overnight campout.**

We went to: _____.

My favorite part was: _____

_____

_____.

Akela's OK   Date   Recorded by the den leader

- **Be prepared:** Talk to Akela about what you need to bring on your outdoor trip.

- **Never go anywhere alone.** Always have a buddy.

- **Always take these eight essentials:**
  1. First aid kit
  2. Filled water bottle
  3. Flashlight
  4. Trail food
  5. Sunscreen
  6. Whistle
  7. Rain gear
  8. Pocketknife

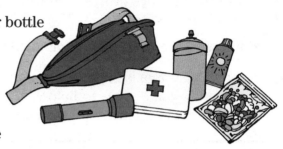

| Akela's OK | Date | Recorded by the den leader |

If You Think You Are Lost

- Stay where you are so rescuers can find you. **Don't try to find your way back.**

- Sit down in the open where people can see you.

- Blow your whistle three times if you hear rescuers.

| Akela's OK | Date | Recorded by the den leader |

d Explain the buddy system.

The Buddy System

- Everyone has a buddy.
- Your buddy goes everywhere with you, and you go everywhere with him.
- Know where your buddy is at all times.

The buddy system is important. If you get hurt or lost, your buddy will be able to help you. Two people can often solve a problem better than one.

 d

_____ _____ _____
Akela's OK   Date   Recorded by the den leader

 e Attend day camp in your area.

e

_____ _____ _____
Akela's OK   Date   Recorded by the den leader

 f Attend resident camp in your area.

f

_____ _____ _____
Akela's OK   Date   Recorded by the den leader

Participate with your den at a campfire in front of your pack.

Campfires are a special time to have fun!

- Sing a fun song that everyone knows. Or teach everyone a simple new song.

- Present a short skit. Make sure that everyone can hear you.

- Tell a joke. It's okay if they have heard it before.

Akela's OK   Date   Recorded by the den leader

 With your den or pack or family, participate in a worship service outdoors.

Akela's OK   Date   Recorded by the den leader

Cub Scout World Conservation Award

The Cub Scout World Conservation Award is an international award you can earn by doing the following things:

Wolf Cub Scouts

_____ Complete Achievement 7.

_____ Complete all Arrow Points in two of the following three electives:

_____ 13. Birds

_____ 15. Grow Something

_____ 19. Fishing

_____ Participate in a den or pack conservation project in addition to the above.

After you have done all of these things, ask your den leader to order your award.

Approved _____

Akela

Cub Scouting's Leave No Trace Award

Leave No Trace is a plan that helps you to be more concerned about your environment. It also helps you protect it for future generations.

You can earn the Cub Scouting's Leave No Trace Award by doing the following things:

1. Discuss with your leader or parent/guardian the importance of the Leave No Trace frontcountry guidelines.
2. On three separate outings, practice the frontcountry guidelines of Leave No Trace.
3. Complete Achievement 7, "Your Living World."
4. Participate in a Leave No Trace–related service project.
5. Promise to practice the Leave No Trace frontcountry guidelines by signing the Cub Scout Leave No Trace Pledge.
6. Draw a poster to illustrate the Leave No Trace frontcountry guidelines and display it at a pack meeting.

Cub Scout Leave No Trace Pledge

I promise to practice the Leave No Trace frontcountry guidelines wherever I go:

1. Plan ahead.
2. Stick to trails.
3. Manage your pet.
4. Leave what you find.
5. Respect other visitors.
6. Trash your trash.

After you have done these things, ask your den leader to order your award.

Approved _____

Akela

NOTE for Akela: Ask your den leader for more information on Cub Scouting's Leave No Trace frontcountry guidelines and this award.

Cub Scout Academics and Sports

You can have fun and learn new skills when you take part in the Cub Scout Academics and Sports program. You can also earn a belt loop just for learning about a sport or academic subject and participating in it. You can take part at home, in your den or pack, or in activities in your community. There are many Academics and Sports subjects for you to choose from.

If you decide to keep on working at an Academics or Sports area over a period of time, you can earn a Cub Scout Academics or Sports pin. The book *Cub Scout Academics and Sports Program Guide* tells you all the requirements you need to know to earn belt loops and pins.

Ask your den leader to tell you more about the Cub Scout Academics and Sports program.

As a Wolf Cub Scout, I have earned these Cub Scout Academics and Sports belt loops:

_____

_____

_____

_____

_____

_____

_____

 Archery

 Art

 Astronomy

 Badminton

 Baseball

 Basketball

 Bicycling

 Bowling

 Chess

 Citizenship

 Collecting

 Communicating

 Computers

 Disabilities Awareness

 Family Travel

 Fishing

 Flag Football

 Geography

 Geology

 Golf

 Good Manners

 Gymnastics

 Heritages

 Hiking

 Hockey

 Horseback Riding

 Kickball

 Ice Skating

 Language and Culture

 Map and Compass

 Marbles

 Mathematics

 Music

 Nutrition

 Pet Care

 Photography

 Physical Fitness

 Reading and Writing

 Roller Skating

 Science

 Skateboarding

 Snow Ski and Board Sports

 Soccer

 Softball

 Swimming

 Table Tennis

 Tennis

 Ultimate

 Video Games

 Volleyball

 Weather

 Wildlife Conservation

Get Set for Bear

When you have finished the second grade (or are 9 years old), you can start working on the achievements and electives in the *Bear Handbook.*

In the *Bear Handbook* you can choose 12 out of 24 achievements to earn your Bear badge. You will have a lot of fun learning about God, your country, your family, and yourself.

You will also have 24 new, fun electives to work on to earn Arrow Points.

Do your best as a Wolf Cub Scout, then join the fun as you work with your family, your den leader, your Cub Scout friends, and Baloo on the Bear Cub Scout trail.

Trail Summary

Your name _____

 BOBCAT TRAIL

 WOLF TRAIL

 ARROW POINT TRAIL

NOTE for Akela: Pages 232–236 may be reproduced when more than one boy is using the book.

Bobcat Trail

Fill in eight tracks to earn the Bobcat badge.

The Cub Scout Promise   1

The Law of the Pack   2

The Meaning of Webelos   3

The Cub Scout Sign   4

The Cub Scout Handshake   5

The Cub Scout Motto   6

The Cub Scout Salute   7

Exercises in *How to Protect Your Children from Child Abuse*   8

Wolf Trail

Fill in the Wolf tracks to show the Wolf achievements you
have completed.

Achievements

1. Feats of Skill

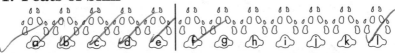

Do ALL of these &   Do ONE of these

2. Your Flag

3. Keep Your Body Healthy

4. Know Your Home and Community

5. Tools for Fixing and Building

6. Start a Collection

7. Your Living World

8. Cooking and Eating

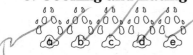

9. Be Safe at Home and on the Street

10. Family Fun

Do THIS ONE &   **Do TWO of these**

11. Duty to God

12. Making Choices

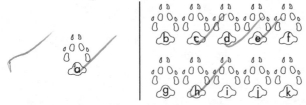

Do THIS ONE &   Do FOUR of these

Arrow Point Trail

Electives

1. It's a Secret (page 110)

a b c d

2. Be an Actor (page 118)

a b c d e

3. Make It Yourself (page 124)

a b c d e

4. Play a Game (page 128)

a b c d e f

5. Spare-Time (page 132)

a b c d e f g h i

6. Books, Books, Books (page 142)

a b c

7. Foot Power (page 146)

a b c

8. Machine Power (page 148)

a b c d

9. Let's Have a Party (page 152)

a b c

10. American Indian Lore (page 154)

a b c d e f

11. Sing-Along (page 162)

a b c d e f

Fill in 10 arrowheads to earn a Gold Arrow Point.

Fill in 10 more arrowheads to earn EACH Silver Arrow Point.

12. Be an Artist (page 168)

a b c d e f

13. Birds (page 174)

a b c d e f

14. Pets (page 178)

a b c d

15. Grow Something (page 184)

a b c d e

16. Family Alert (page 188)

a b c

17. Tie It Right (page 190)

a b c d e f g

18. Outdoor Adventure (page 196)

a b c d e f g

19. Fishing (page 200)

a b c d e f

20. Sports (page 204)

a b c d e f g h i j
k l m n o

21. Computers (page 216)

a b c

22. Say It Right (page 218)

a b c d e

23. Let's Go Camping (page 222)

a b c d e f g h